BUILDING
a MAGICAL
RELATIONSHIP

BUILDING A MAGICAL RELATIONSHIP

The Five Points of Love

CYNTHIA JANE COLLINS
and JANE RAEBURN

May you be thrice blessed!
Jane Raeburn

CITADEL PRESS
Kensington Publishing Corp.
www.kensingtonbooks.com

CITADEL PRESS BOOKS are published by

Kensington Publishing Corp.
850 Third Avenue
New York, NY 10022

All Kensington titles, imprints, and distributed lines are available at special quantity discounts for bulk purchases for sales promotions, premiums, fund-raising, educational, or institutional use. Special book excerpts or customized printings can also be created to fit specific needs. For details, write or phone the office of the Kensington special sales manager: Kensington Publishing Corp., 850 Third Avenue, New York, NY 10022, attn: Special Sales Department, phone 1-800-221-2647.

Citadel Press and the Citadel Logo are trademarks of Kensington Publishing Corp.

Tarot drawings by Cynthia Jane Collins, after Pamela Coleman Smith

First printing: February 2002

10 9 8 7 6 5 4 3 2 1

Printed in the United States of America

Library of Congress Control Number: 2001098931

ISBN: 0-8065-2306-9

Text design: Stanley S. Drate/Folio Graphics Co. Inc.

*This book is for Cassius,
Harry, and Chris,
who taught us what
good relationships are.*

Contents

Preface

Real Ideas for Real Partners

This is a book for Wiccans and Pagans. Our religions are growing, changing, and in some ways maturing, and so are we. Many of us value the way our spirituality guides and sustains us in dealing with the problems of adulthood, including forming and sustaining good relationships.

This is also a book for people who aren't Wiccan or Pagan. Perhaps you're involved with someone who follows one of these spiritual paths, or perhaps you're just interested in a different perspective on some familiar issues.

Whoever you are, we welcome you to these pages and hope that you find something of value here. In this introduction, we'll show you some of the tools we intend to use throughout the book. First, though, we'd like to introduce ourselves.

WHO WE ARE

We are two Wiccans who currently enjoy delightful relationships. To get here, we each had to do a lot of work and go through some painful experiences.

When we decided to write this book, we took a great deal of time to discuss what we wanted it to be. We carefully looked at what knowledge and experience each of us would bring to the process.

―――――――――――――― *Cynthia Speaks* ――――――――――

When I was a little girl, I was intrigued with Halloween. It is very close to my birthday, and it was a wonderful chance to get dressed up and experience things in a new and different way. I could be a queen, a dancer, or even a witch. The pirates and goblins scared some of my friends, but I wasn't scared. I knew they were good people just pretending to be bad. They would take off their costumes and go back to being good people. What frightened me when I was little, and still frightens me today, are people who appear good on the outside, but are sick inside. Because I grew up in an alcoholic and sexually abusive home, I learned a lot about the difference between what is on the outside and what is on the inside.

The things I bring to this book are directly from my experience. I've been involved in three marriages that ended in divorce. I have done a whole lot wrong and learned from it.

My first three marriages began full of hope and promise. They ended with me full of resentment and confusion. I was miserable. I didn't see what I had done to deserve this! I found a lot of help and personal growth in twelve-step recovery programs, and I practice those steps to this day. Through this work, I came to realize that there was still something seriously unhappy inside me. I eventually went into therapy and spent several years working on sexual abuse issues from my family.

My fourth marriage—to Chris, whom I had known since high school—was healthy and happy even though he died a lingering and horrible death. I am now married again, and using the Principles we discuss in this book, Harry and I have a strong and loving relationship.

I began my spiritual journey with the Catholic Church, and during the 1960s investigated the Eastern disciplines, Judaism, and feminist spirituality. Over time, I identified with a number of groups and traditions, finding a piece of myself in each. I've been a practicing solitary witch (though I did not know the name for it until the 1980s) for most of my life. In 1994, I helped found a Coven of Elders, the Circle of the Silver Cauldron, and am still a part of that coven.

I was so serious about my explorations of spirituality that I studied for a master of divinity degree, specializing in early church history and pastoral care and counseling. I spent two years as a pastor for the United Methodist Church and during that time completed a master's degree in counseling, focusing on abuse and abuse-related issues, including chemical dependency, sexual abuse, and domestic violence.

I am a clinical member of the American Association for Marriage and Family Therapy, and a licensed therapist in Maine. I am also a professional visual artist, teacher, mother of three grown children, and author of *Vacation Pagan School,* a training program for newcomers to Pagan religions.

Jane Speaks

I started reading when I was three, wrote my first poem when I was four, and began my journalism career when I was nineteen. In 1991 I was initiated as a Wiccan and began writing "Jane's Tidings," a column of Pagan-related news that appeared in several magazines over the next seven years. I then began work on a book, which became *Celtic Wicca: Ancient Wisdom for the 21st Century.*

Around that time, I was doing a lot of thinking about relationships. Trying to get away from an unhappy situation, I had abruptly left a partner of several years for another man. The new liaison didn't last, and I found myself alone and still unhappy. I realized I had a lot to learn before I could conduct a relationship successfully.

I started reading experts' work on relationships. Though my research helped me understand my own mistakes better, I also noticed that much of the available material had a distinctly Christian slant. This ranged from benign ("Ask God to help you communicate better") to some that was difficult to take seriously ("Wives should submit to their husbands"). I respect Christianity, but it's not my religion, and I found its teachings on relationships weren't always relevant to my spiritual outlook.

During that sad time, it occurred to me that a book about Pagans' relationships could be useful and valuable. I recognized that my own limited knowledge wasn't going to be enough to complete the project, so I set the idea aside.

In time, I became closer friends with Cassius, an intelligent and charming man whom I'd known slightly for years. We shared a religion, an interest in books and history, and a silly sense of humor. Over the next few years we fell in love, moved in together, and were married. I applied some of the knowledge I'd gained, and together we enjoy a delightful, loving, and spiritual partnership.

Cynthia and I met by chance soon after she moved to the town where I live. We became good friends, and we learned about each other's knowledge and interest in this subject. I brought up my old idea and together we created the book you're reading. Our work together has deepened our friendship and mutual respect.

As we strove to get the project started, we did a ritual asking for Divine help in making this book honorable, useful, and beautiful. (We'll let you decide if we succeeded.) As part of the spellwork, we made bread and offered it at the beach, then looked for rocks to take home as symbols of the work in progress. As we hunted, Cynthia found a ten-dollar bill on the sand, which we spent on some yummy food. We thought it was a good sign. It's not every day that the Divine Ones take you out to lunch!

Acknowledgments

We would like to thank, in alphabetical order: Karen Albin Edmonds for editorial advice and for being Cynthia's best cousin, Pat Arant for advice on Marya Morevna, Charles Ashanin for patience and love, Connie Bredestege for being a friend for more than forty years, Nancy Gardella for the "spiritual" help, Bill Keith for encouragement and information, Heather Keith for proofreading, Nina Keith for being a sister, Lilith McClelland for listening, Joy Piland for proofreading, Dave Plottel for the Crock-Pot and the rotten hut, Eric Robbins and Rita Moran at Apple Valley Books for their wise counsel, Kerry Robinson for proofreading, Heather Sargent for helping a blocked artist, the Terrible Trio (Steffan, Stephanie, and Jess) for their energy and life, Margaret Wolf at Citadel for her patience and help, and Cynthia's children for putting up with her as she struggled to put these Principles to work.

We also thank all those who have provided us with the opportunity to grow, and all those who encouraged us as this book became a reality, including past and present members of the Tuesday Night Tarot group, Temple of Brigantia, Circle of the Silver Cauldron, Vacation Pagan School, EarthTides Pagan Network, and the Maine Pagan Mailing List.

Finally, we thank Divine Ones for lunch and inspiration, our husbands for countless acts of support and love, and each other for being the best coauthors ever!

BUILDING
A MAGICAL
RELATIONSHIP

Introduction

Paganism 101

In case you're new to all this, a quick overview: "Pagan" and "Neopagan" religions are a group of faiths that vary widely, generally based on reverence for nature, respect for individual freedom, and a hearkening back to pre-Christian gods and goddesses. By far the largest religion within this category is called Wicca, or modern Witchcraft. In this book, we'll use a lot of concepts from Wicca, but please know that not all Pagans adhere to these specific ideas.

What is different about the way Pagans view relationships, as opposed to the way other religions do? To start with, Pagan religions generally honor healthy sexuality as a part of the natural world, sacred rather than dirty or shameful. "All acts of love and pleasure are My rituals," says a Goddess in one of the best-known Wiccan texts. Thoughtful Pagans realize that the sacred nature of sexuality means it is an affront to the Divine to treat this gift irresponsibly.

Pagans believe in the right to choose your own path, provided you do not harm others. Each person is responsible for his or her own sexuality and has free will in choosing when, how, and with whom to express it. This leads to a remarkable diversity in our relationships. Most Pagans are accepting of same-sex unions and various forms of "polyamory," or arrangements in which a person might have more than one partner. Many Pagans are more conventional in their choices, and their path is honored as well.

Also, Pagans aren't obligated to remain together for a lifetime. Many do so, of course. Others follow a tradition of "handfasting," or choosing a partner for a specific time, usually a year, after which the partners decide together to continue or part.

As authors, we bring our own differing choices to this book. When Jane and Cassius were married, they chose each other as exclusive partners with a lifetime commitment. Cynthia and Harry's vows joined them for "as long as our love shall last," and they have an agreement that allows the possibility of secondary partners outside their primary relationship. (More on this in chapter 5 on Balance.)

Finally, most Pagans view the sexes as equal in value and potential. They do not believe either sex is divinely ordained to act any particular role. Men and women have the freedom to invent and choose their own lives, as well as the responsibility to accept the consequences of their choices.

In this book, our goal is to encourage healthy, lasting relationships, whatever form they may take. You may face issues that are specific to your situation, but the principles of a healthy relationship are the same.

Most of the examples in this book involve couples. Does this mean we're excluding people who are polyamorous? No. If you have two partners, you have two relationships. You cannot control how those partners relate to one another; the only thing you can work on is how you relate to each of them. So the more partners you have, the more necessary "couples" skills are.

If you are not partnered, you may still find this book helpful. If you are seeking a partner, the skills and tools here can help you recognize healthy patterns and spend your energy and time with people whose actions are worthy of your respect. If you have chosen to remain single, for a time or for life, know that the information here can be applied to many types of interactions—even your relationship with yourself.

A Quartered Circle

This book is founded on five Principles. We like to envision them as four quarters of a circle, with Balance in the center. This visualization echoes the points of a Wiccan circle, in which participants usually honor the four compass directions and the center as having specific energies and powers.

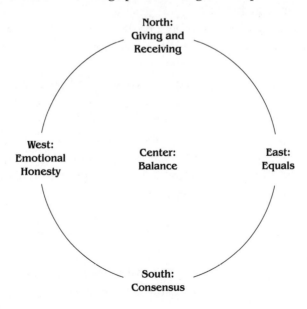

North:
Giving and
Receiving

West:
Emotional
Honesty

Center:
Balance

East:
Equals

South:
Consensus

These Principles are time-tested concepts for evaluating, understanding, and improving a relationship.

- **The Principle of Equals.**   No partner in a relationship is to be considered inferior or superior. My wants, needs and fears are no more or less important, though they may at times be more or less urgent, than those of my partner. We both deserve time, energy, and resources.
- **The Principle of Consensus.**   We choose our path together. We both agree on choices that are for both of us, and when we do not agree, we do not follow that path until we are in agreement. We commit to discussing and wrestling with our hopes and fears, wants and needs, money, power, and sexuality. We don't try to manipulate each other.
- **The Principle of Emotional Honesty.**   We are emotionally honest with ourselves and each other. We commit to being open to change, to the process of facing and accepting uncomfortable emotions in ourselves and each other. We tell each other the truth about ourselves, even when it is difficult.
- **The Principle of Giving and Receiving.**   We freely give and freely receive. Neither of us owes the other. What we do, we do because we choose.
- **The Principle of Balance.**   We choose how our relationship will balance with the other aspects of our lives. We consider how much time, energy, and resources we are willing to invest in each other. We balance all the Principles against one another, finding ways to be loving while being honest, to give and receive freely while maintaining equality and consensus.

Tools for Growth

We'll explore each Principle in its own section of this book. Because different people learn in different ways, we've chosen to work with the Principles using several tools.

First among these is storytelling. Each chapter includes stories from world mythology, from our personal experiences, and from our imaginations, intended to show the Principles in action. Cynthia focuses on a relationship that stayed strong despite the strain of her husband's terminal illness. Jane balances this with stories from day-to-day situations.

The myths are used as myths have been used throughout history, to illuminate our experiences and provide explanations for life's mysteries. Though we've retold them in our own words, we've tried to be respectful of the cultures from which they came, to present these stories without altering their main points.

In the fictional examples that we use in these pages, the names and situations of the partners are not intended to depict any specific real-life problem or person. They are meant to be stories of people we may recognize from our modern lives.

One couple, George and Vicki, face a situation that requires working through each of the Principles, and their story continues throughout the book. Other partners' difficulties reach some kind of resolution within each section.

Second, we describe exercises you can try, by yourself or with a partner. It may feel silly or meaningless to do one of these at first, but they are based on standard therapeutic techniques and are designed to help you gain insight about yourself and your relationship.

We also rely on divination (specifically, Tarot cards) and spellwork to help draw spirituality into the healing process. These are offered as tools, which you can—and should—choose and adapt as you see fit. The object of the Tarot reading is not to "tell fortunes," but to shed light on a situation and suggest areas to explore. Our readings are based on a standard seventy-eight card deck; in this book you'll see Cynthia's illustrations, adapted from the well-known "Rider-Waite" cards. We encourage you to use any deck that appeals to you.

Why use Tarot? First, because many Pagans are already familiar with it. Second, in some situations the cards are useful as a "third party" in a discussion, providing a way to raise and talk about issues in ways that are less likely to be perceived as attacks. Finally, people who understand information visually may find value in meditating on the card images when words are unclear.

If you don't feel comfortable using Tarot cards, you might try asking a trusted friend to offer his or her views on each of the topics covered by the card positions in the spread.

Each chapter has its own Tarot spread, and the readings we've done for the characters in the stories are real—that is, we didn't decide ahead of time what the cards were going to say. We simply shuffled a deck, focused on the story, laid out the cards, and wrote down whatever came up. Some of the readings couldn't have been more appropriate if we had prearranged them!

Finally, each chapter includes rituals or spells. These are a standard component of Pagan worship. In relationships in which the partners are open to this sort of work, rituals help to add a spiritual dimension to agreements, shared goals, problem solving, and the simple expression of love. "Spells" are at their root a form of prayer, often with a physical object as a symbol. We find them valuable for reinforcing our intentions and asking divine aid in carrying out those intentions.

At the end of the book (appendix) you'll find—another book! *The Relationship Spellbook* contains the full text of all the exercises, spells, and rituals of the main book in a format you can use for yourself.

Spellwork for Beginners

If you're not familiar with Wiccan and Pagan forms of prayer, worship, and self-work, here are a few concepts that will help you understand the spells and rituals here:

Visualization/Imagination.   In some ways, this is the same skill you used when you played "pretend" games as a child. As an adult, you might use this skill to mentally decorate a room or imagine your future life. For Pagans, it is a spiritual skill, part of our way of praying, and a useful way to practice "psychic" skills. For people of many spiritual paths, it is part of meditation and relaxation, and is also useful for problem solving and connecting with the Divine.

Altars.   The idea of setting aside space to honor the Divine and express your spiritual ideas dates back centuries. An altar need not be elaborate—it can be the top of a bureau, or even the earth itself.

"So mote it be."   An archaic way of saying "It is so" or "So be it." Wiccans use this as an emphatic way of ending a ritual or piece of a ritual, much as Christians use "Amen."

Projective/Receptive Hand.   Many Wiccans learn in their training that one hand (usually the one you write with) is "projective," better suited to symbolic acts of sending energy outward, while the other is "receptive," better suited to drawing energies inward.

Circle/Sacred Space.   Before engaging in a prayer or ritual, many Pagans use objects, motions and words to declare an ordinary space—often, but not always, a circle—to be sacred. This is a way of mentally and emotionally setting yourself outside daily distractions to bring your most thoughtful, spiritual side to whatever you're doing.

Calling the Quarters.   Many Wiccans, after establishing sacred space, honor the energies associated with the four compass directions and the center. The idea of these energies comes from medieval ceremonial magic. This "calling the quarters" serves to reinforce the protection of the space and establish a sense of balance in the participant. The quartered circle also serves as the framework for this book.

What if you're not Pagan, or don't find spells and rituals meaningful? There is absolutely no requirement that you use these tools to have a happy, healthy relationship. You may wish to look over *The Relationship Spellbook* in the appendix anyway. Some of the "rituals" there are drawn from time-tested concepts used by therapists and may be beneficial once you have adapted them to suit the spiritual paths of the people involved.

We do suggest that finding shared spiritual ground with your partner is beneficial, even if you simply agree to enjoy walking on the beach together. Bringing your spiritual self to a partner, in whatever way is right for you, is a powerful act of trust and can build a stronger connection.

For Pagans, spiritual acts are also acts of creativity. Generally Pagan rituals are crafted by the people who perform them, not handed down in a "holy book." We offer the rituals in the Spellbook in the hope and expectation that you will use them as a source of ideas, adapting them to your own needs and style rather than performing them word for word.

If you would like to try spells and rituals, but have not done so in the past, here are some starting points to think about: Make sure your surroundings are physically comfortable, including temperature, privacy, and clothing. Use sounds and smells to create a calm, focused mood. Be aware of nature, and evoke your connection to it using words, objects, and images. If you'd like to explore more before you try the rituals here, we'll suggest other useful resources at the end of the book.

Basic Relationship Skills

As we were writing this book, we sought ideas and feedback from a number of helpful friends. One friend, after reading chapter 1 on the Principle of Equals, began thinking about her marriage of many years, and realized, "Oh! I don't *have* a relationship!" Time and tradition had set her and her husband in a pattern so strong that he had no idea what she thought or felt, and undoing that pattern was a turbulent process for them both. Ultimately her realization set them on their way to a better understanding of each other.

From her experience, we realized that some elementary communication skills will be helpful as you apply the Principles. You need not be perfect in all these skills. These are things we work on every day. Look at this list as a source of ideas for breaking down barriers between you and a partner.

Speaking for yourself.   We often find ourselves wanting to make a statement, and instead we ask a question or offer advice. We are tempted to ask our relationship partner, "How can you only sleep five hours and still do a full day's work?" or to say, "You need to get more sleep." It is difficult to learn to say instead, "My experience is that I don't do well unless I get eight hours of sleep a night."

Listening and hearing.   We have all been in conversations that seemed to go nowhere, or that dragged on until someone "won." One partner doesn't seem to understand what the other is trying to communicate. Too often we are listening with our defensive shields up, set to catch and counter any misspoken word, rather than to hear and understand. The ability to say "I understand" before "I wish to respond" is the essence of this skill.

Recognizing your own emotions.   We are human, which means we receive input from the world around us through our bodies. Our bodies always produce emotions when they interact with our world or our own imaginations. Emotions allow us access to senses beyond the rational and logical. What we do with and about our emotions helps determine success in relationships.

We often trade away important parts of ourselves—our emotions, our preferences, our ethics—just to keep the supposed peace. This skill is about recognizing and naming your feelings and making choices that acknowledge them, to express them in ways that help to improve the situation. A lot of addictive and abusive behavior comes from being afraid to know and honor our own strong feelings.

The positive side of this skill has to do with recognizing and celebrating the times when we feel joy, passion, love, triumph, or any number of feelings. This is vital to a loving relationship, for the expression of these feelings together is a powerful bond.

Putting your thoughts and feelings into words.   This is tough for many people, especially those who got the message early in life that their feelings were "bad" or "wrong." Often as children we learned to hide our feelings to protect ourselves or others, but lost a bit of our identity in the process. You'll learn more about this in chapter 3 on Emotional Honesty. For now, if you don't feel comfortable talking seriously with a partner, think about when the problem started, and what each of you could do differently to make communication less of a struggle.

Grounding.   This Wiccan term refers to a time of quiet and calm during which you relax and focus to clear your mind of anxiety and distractions. This time of meditation or contemplation can be seen in the services of many religions, and many physicians recommend it for reducing stress. Most Pagans ground themselves before rituals, often spending this time focusing on their own connection to the earth. For many people, simply being still and taking a few deep breaths can help relieve anxiety and gain clarity. You may also wish to try the

"Grounding Meditation" found in the appendix, *The Relationship Spellbook.*

Realistic expectations. We all go through life with incomplete information. To help us fill in the gaps in our knowledge, we make assumptions and set expectations based on the information we do have. Those assumptions may be based on bad information or may just be wrong for the situation where we try to apply them. This skill is about recognizing when something we believe to be true is based on fact or on assumptions, and about knowing when to check out our beliefs before acting on them.

One way to look at this is to remember that C is a passing grade. If we try to get straight A's in every aspect of our lives, or if we expect that of a partner, we will be doomed to disappointment. Few things really require or deserve our 100 percent effort. It is unrealistic to expect that a house with two working adults will be completely neat at all times, or that nothing will go wrong on our wedding day, or that the checkbook will always balance to the penny. We can easily find ourselves "majoring in the minors," getting upset about things that will not matter in a week. If this is happening to you, start by taking a look at the assumptions you've made about yourself and your life.

Working Alone

The only person you can change is yourself. For that reason, many of the exercises in this book can be done alone. We realize that sometimes, despite sincere effort and intention, we may not be able to engage a partner in the work of strengthening our relationship.

If this is the case, the partner may be getting his or her needs met by the way things are going now and may find changes uncomfortable. Self-improvement is not easy for the fearful. It may be that the partner is not as committed to the relationship. Or a partner may have another situation (work, illness, another love, addictions) eating up time and energy.

Reading this book will not change your partner's character or bring you the perfect lover. We hope you will find help here to see your situation more clearly, including the ways you have contributed to its patterns, good and bad. Even if you and your partner are both actively involved in building a better relationship, you may still find value in doing some of the exercises alone. This gives you time to think about what you learned before sharing it.

Whatever your partner's attitude, we caution you to be careful not to let these possibilities blind you to your own growth and change. Are you becoming deeper, stronger, less critical and controlling, more ethical as you make these changes? Is your character reflecting more of love, healthy boundaries, and compassion? Would you like to be around the person you are becoming?

One place to start: Take responsibility for your body. This can be as simple as paying more attention to personal hygiene and grooming. Any medical issue that gets in the way of being fully present in your relationship—birth control, addiction, back problems, depression—needs to be evaluated by a professional. Your best efforts to be attentive to your partner will be impaired if you are not sleeping at night or your teeth hurt or you are hungover.

Find caregivers you trust and get the treatment you need. Make a healthy lifestyle a priority and a treat for yourself. As we discuss in chapter 5 on Balance, anger and other emotions come from your body, and giving your body the best possible attention is a first step toward honoring and understanding your emotions.

When to Get Help

In some situations, a book is not enough. As we discuss in chapter 2 on Consensus, there are some people with whom it is simply not possible to have the type of healthy relationship that is the goal of this book.

On your side, if you find that repeated efforts to change a pattern aren't working, or that you consistently get in your own way whenever you try to honestly explore past issues and present patterns, it may be time to enlist the help of a third party. Sometimes simply talking to someone whose opinion you respect can give you enough perspective to make changes. At times, though, it may be important to seek help from either a peer support group (such as Adult Children of Alcoholics, Debtors Anonymous, or a sexual crisis recovery group) or from a trained professional, or both.

Some behaviors indicate a problem requiring specialized help. Addiction, abuse, and violence, in your current family or in your family of origin, leave deep scars and drain away your creativity, your life force, and your personal reserves. Simply choosing to be different is a step forward, but it is not enough unless the roots of the problem are addressed. A combination of peer support and professional help is the best.

At the bottom of violent and addictive patterns is a desire to control and exercise power over others while avoiding responsibility for oneself. Look at the two questions below. If you answer yes to any part of them, then it is time to get additional help. You can't handle it alone. No one can. You're not "crazy" if you get counseling to deal with these issues. On the contrary, getting help when you need it is a sign of mental health.

Are you afraid around your partner? This includes the sense that you have to "walk on eggshells" with your partner. This feeling might be because of physical or sexual coercion, aggressive (yelling, put-downs, loud noises) or passive (pouting, sabotaging, minimizing) control, isolation, intimidation, threats, deprivation, or emotional, spiritual, or economic abuse.

Do you find yourself doing things or thinking about things without being able to stop, despite your best efforts? This includes, but is not limited to, exaggerated levels of:

- Spending, saving, or not meeting your financial obligations
- Bingeing, purging, or refusing food
- Sexual acting out or withdrawing
- Re-feeling old angers, fears, or resentments
- Feeling out of control
- Sleeping too much or too little
- Risky or self-destructive behaviors: smoking, using drugs or alcohol, driving unsafely, suicidal thoughts, self-injury
- Feeling anxious most of the time
- Avoidance behaviors: excessive TV, reading, playing on the computer, "addiction" to a hobby or sport
- Constantly criticizing yourself or others

It is possible to work on a relationship while getting help with one or more of these problems. It is *not* possible to establish lasting improvement in the relationship without addressing these behaviors when they are present.

Begin the Journey

The information in this book reflects the views of just two Pagans. We do not claim to represent everyone who follows these paths, nor do we say that our way is the only right one. The ideas we offer here are based on our experience and training, and we believe they can be adapted to work in virtually any situation. Still, we encourage you to evaluate our ideas thoughtfully and apply them in the way that's best for you.

Our experience is that each individual is valuable and worthy. That presumption carries with it a great deal of freedom and a great deal of responsibility. Pagans believe we are ultimately, radically responsible for what we do, how we do it, when we do it, and with what intention.

It is in conflict that the true test of our ethics emerges.

There can be no ethical choice unless there is a genuine choice. Making such choices help us become better people and better partners.

We wish you learning and growth in your seeking and your choosing, and love and happiness in the journey.

Knowing Your Own Mind

The Principle of Equals

The mind and the heart are closely intertwined. In starting with the East—associated in various traditions with the element of air, with communication, new beginnings, and mental energy—we honor the thinking that goes into building a good relationship, and we offer some tools for focusing your own thoughts. For until you understand yourself, you cannot truly let a partner understand you.

One of the central ideas most Wiccans and Pagans share is that partners in a relationship should be equal. Though we may assume different roles (breadwinner, stay-at-home parent, social director, home maintenance engineer), there is no assumption in modern Pagan religions that either gender is subservient, or that there are divinely ordained privileges for the person who fills one role or another. We begin by focusing on this Principle of Equals, both as a starting ground for building a relationship and as a framework for better understanding your own choices:

> **We honor one another as equals.** My wants and needs, hopes and fears are no more or less important, though they may at times be more or less urgent, than those of my partner. We both deserve time, energy, and resources.

The idea of equals is one of fairness in a larger sense than one for one. I buy us lunch one week, and you buy it the next. Sounds fair, right? But if every time I buy we eat drive-through hamburgers, while you always pay for "Chez Expensive," we need to check on whether that says "equals" to us. And maybe it does! I may have a limited income while you have a great job.

If every time we get together, we only talk about your problems, and you are not paying me as your counselor, this probably isn't equal in terms of time. If you always give me a back rub or a Reiki session, and I don't offer to return the favor, it might be well to raise the question of how the energy in our relationship is being shared.

Myth: The Divided Daughter

Hades, the Greek Lord of the Underworld, had perhaps a textbook case of "equals": His wife, Persephone, spent half the year in the underworld with him, and half the year on earth with her mother Demeter, goddess of grain.

Hades had started this relationship by abducting Persephone, and he was pretty sure this entitled him to keep her all to himself. Demeter grieved for her daughter and refused to bring springtime to the land for many months until Hades agreed to the half-and-half arrangement.

The Greeks who wrote the myths were more concerned about explaining the seasons than about Persephone's marital struggles. No one seems to have asked her where *she* wanted to be! But the balancing act—struggling to give proper amounts of love, time, and energy both to a partner and to a parent—is as old as time.

Most of us wouldn't be content with a relationship in which our partner left every spring to spend six months at Mom's. But it seems to be working for them. After all, we still get fresh flowers and grain every summer!

EQUAL BUT INDIVIDUAL

True equality requires recognizing each other's preferences, personalities, and thoughts. If both partners take twenty dollars a week from the family budget for lunch, that may sound equal, but it may not take into account what is available for lunch close to work, or individual dietary choices. For one person, going with a partner to a wedding may be a minor inconvenience, a nice gift of time. For another person, who happens to be painfully shy, the same gift may represent a major sacrifice.

It's easy to come up with examples for the idea that one partner's needs may be more urgent than another's. For example, my broken arm is more time-sensitive than my partner's desire to watch *Lost in Space* reruns. But is my battle with monthly blahs more urgent than my partner's desire to bring me to his child's softball game? If my partner enjoys doing counted cross-stitch—a time-consuming but fairly inexpensive hobby—while I like playing "House of the Dead" at the arcade at forty dollars for thirty minutes, are we honoring the idea of equals?

Myth: Macha the Swift

In many ways, ancient cultures did not accept the idea that people in a marriage or other relationships were equals. Yet the Principle of balancing needs and resources between partners was well established, illustrated in myth in often dramatic ways.

In the eighth century—after Christianity had taken a firm hold in Ireland, but perhaps close enough to the Pagan era to reflect some of that ancient time's lore and religion—there was written the story of Macha. Among the women of her world she had status and talent, for she was a rich landlord's wife, known for her ability to manage his household.

Crunniuc, her husband, went one day to a fair, where all the people of Ulster gathered. As he departed, Macha warned him not to be boastful or careless. (Perhaps she knew the ale would be plentiful!) As is the way in these stories, he forgot the warning. At the end of the day's racing, he boasted that his wife could run faster than the king's chariot and horses. Apparently he made quite a noise about it, for royal messengers were sent to fetch her—and did not take no for an answer, even though it was clear she was heavily pregnant.

She tried to refuse, naturally enough. When she finally agreed to run the race, she vowed that a long-lasting evil would come on the men of Ulster for making her do it. She won, as promised, then immediately gave birth to twins. In her pain, she let out a scream and a curse: All the men who heard her scream, the men who could have stopped the race, would suffer the most painful pangs of childbirth for five days and four nights at their time of greatest difficulty. And they did, and so did their children, for nine generations.

This was a classic case of urgency. Crunniuc may have sought status in his community by boasting of his wife's abilities, and under some circumstances she might have been pleased to help his efforts. But this was obviously not the moment! Women in ancient Ireland may not have been equal to men, but the tellers of tales knew it was foolish to demand their utter subjection to men's every whim.

THE GOLDEN PILLOWS

Often, "equals" questions can be broken down into three basic areas: material resources, energy, and time. The Principle of Equals is about overall balance. We recognize that energy, time, and resources are finite. We cannot act to bring them into balance unless we are aware of our own needs, thoughts, feelings, hopes, and fears, and then those of our partner.

This notion of equals is much easier to implement at the start of a relationship but can and should be revisited often during a lasting union. The simple idea "we are equals" becomes more difficult when relationships and boundaries change, as they inevitably will. What was equal in one context often is not equal in another, and no partner should expect a single negotiation to establish eternal equality. We realize that so much time or so much energy is fairly traded for so much resource, but it's often hard to recognize when it's time to sit down and rebalance the scales. For example, the following couple is working on deeper equality as their relationship matures.

Maude, thirty-four, a lawyer, and Eleanor, thirty, a freelance designer, had been partners for almost four years. They were very conscious of the challenges that face same-sex couples, especially Wiccan ones. They both had good communication skills and were committed to deepening their relationship. When they decided to buy a condominium together, they agreed that Maude who made more money, would contribute most of the monthly payment for the first two years, which would allow Eleanor to establish herself in her profession.

Maude came home one evening, threw down her briefcase, put her hands on her hips, and gave a Look of Death, saying, "What is the meaning of THAT?" Eleanor was mystified. The seeming cause of Maude's outburst was two new sofa pillows. Eleanor had been looking for just the perfect pillows for some time. The two had talked it over, and Eleanor had chosen the golden color to honor Maude's affinity with the lion totem. The pillows were attractive, in keeping with their decor and their budget.

What was the problem? As is often the case with strong rushes of feeling, Maude's emotion over the pillows reflected a much deeper issue. She had been working long hours, and though she'd talked with Eleanor about what to buy, Maude hadn't been there to make the final choice. This aggravated Maude's feeling of being excluded from decisions about "her" home. Eleanor was feeling guilty about her unequal contribution and thought she'd done Maude a favor by taking care of the purchase, trying to "even things up" by doing errands while Maude was at work.

Every relationship is in constant change. The shifts can be very difficult to spot, because when we live with one another, we make assumptions based on our past experiences. The assumptions are often made with the best of all possible motives, both for our good and for our partner's. Eleanor saw herself as giving her artistic and shopping talents to the relationship, taking care of mundane details that might eat up Maude's precious free time. Further, she took into account Maude's preferences to make a statement about her love for her partner. Perhaps Eleanor was even psychically picking up on Maude's desire to be more represented in the home.

What happened was subtle. The needs, wants, thoughts, and feelings of the couple, as measured by time, energy, and resources, were not being given equal weight. Maude felt she didn't have enough time to enjoy her home and her relationship, while Eleanor felt guilty for the free time she had and the extra material resources Maude's job made possible. Eleanor expended energy to make up for the time and money, and Maude felt resentful because she didn't have an equal amount of energy to give.

On the surface, Maude and Eleanor were not aware of what was happening. They had discussed the big changes, such as buying the condominium, and had negotiated potential problems, such as the inequality in financial resources. The other things—the growing sense of distance Maude was experiencing because of her work, and the growing discomfort Eleanor was experiencing because of her lesser financial contribution—crept up slowly. The explosion over the sofa pillows simply exposed undercurrents.

To help her focus on the real issue, Maude did the Clarifying Questions exercise that follows. Note how her answers quickly move away from the fight with Eleanor and into Maude's own problems of balancing her life.

Describe the situation in words.   "I came home and basically lost it. Eleanor bought new pillows for the couch and it was the final straw. I feel like I never have a say in my home. This is the first time I've actually owned my own place."

Who is involved?   "Eleanor, me."

What is happening?   "I don't have the time to do everything I want to do."

Where is this happening?   "At home. At work."

When does this happen?   "I only blow up if I let things build up without saying anything."

How does this happen?   "I come home, expecting to relax and enjoy being with my love, and something hits me the wrong way."

Why does this happen?   "I may be a bit touchy. If I've been in court all day, it's worse. I'm paid to pick at everyone and everything for my clients."

What do I want?   "I want to be able to feel like I am really a part of the loving couple we are, especially at home."

If I could wave my magic wand, what would happen?   "There would be a magic waterfall at the doorway to our home that would wash away all the lawyer stuff, and Eleanor and I would just be face to face."

What would I do?   "I'd stop being so hateful."

What would others do? "Eleanor would be more aware of my stresses, and we would keep more up-to-date on where each of us is emotionally."

How would the situation change? "I'd feel more connected to my home."

What is the very best thing that could possibly happen here? "We'd really be partners, in all areas, like we really want to be."

What do I think? "I think I'm working too hard."

What is my opinion? "I believe that I'd better let Eleanor know what's going on with me."

Who is right? "We both are."

Who is wrong? "Mostly me, but Eleanor can be pretty pushy."

What do I think is likely in this situation? "I think we'll be able to get our act together because we have a strong bond."

What has happened like this in the past? "The only thing I can think of was when my sister (she was just five or six) got into my makeup and used it on her dolls. I was maybe fifteen or sixteen. I was furious. My mother said that since I had gotten involved in track at school, I wasn't spending as much time with my sister, and she was just trying to get my attention. I thought she was just a spoiled brat."

What do I feel? What are my emotions? "I feel invaded and irritated with Eleanor and myself. I am frustrated that I don't have more time but determined to fix what's wrong."

What do I need? "I need to be a part of the household, of my partner's life."

What is the worst thing that could happen and how would it affect me? "I think the worst thing would be if I let a little thing like this drive a wedge between us. But the second worst would be to let things like this go until they become resentments. The worst would pretty much be me being a control freak, a stress addict, and not being truthful with Eleanor."

What are the things I have control over? "I can change how

I deal with stress. I can change how I act when I get home. I can be open with Eleanor."

What are the things I don't have control over?   "I can't control my trial schedule, since I'm not even a junior partner yet. I can't control what Eleanor does with her day. I can't control Eleanor."

What reality has to shift for my intention to be manifest?   "I would have to be more in the good reality where Eleanor and I are partners, and our work enriches us as individuals rather than driving us apart."

How can I bring that about through correspondences?   "I could do some breathing and body de-stress exercises. I could do something symbolic to leave my work stresses at work and not let them into the house. I could ask Eleanor to do some spellwork with me to help me feel a part of our home."

In this exercise, Maude discovered that there was a direct connection between her activity at work and her short temper at home. She also noted that she hadn't been giving Eleanor good information about what was important to her. She reaffirmed how important partnership and home were for her.

She took one image from her exercise and made it a part of her home. With Eleanor's permission, Maude chose and hung a painting of a waterfall in the entryway to their condo, to remind her to leave her work stresses outside.

Next, she turned to the Equals Tarot Spread (see appendix) to get ideas for how to reestablish equality in their relationship.

The cards in the center represent Maude's Self (upper) and her true situation (lower). She first looked at the Self card, which in this case is the Lovers, one of the Major Arcana. (The standard Tarot deck is divided into the Major Arcana—a set of twenty-two individual cards bearing Roman numerals and depicting stages in an initiate's journey—and the Minor Ar-

cana, organized into four fourteen-card suits: Swords, Wands, Cups, and Pentacles.)

As the next step in the reading, Maude looked to see if there were any other cards in the reading that matched her Self card by number or suit. The Lovers is card VI, so she looked for sixes, and the Major Arcana count as a fifth suit, so she looked for other Major Arcana cards. Finally, she looked at the cards opposite the matching ones.

There is one other 6, of Cups, in the position representing Maude's energy. The other Major Arcana card in this reading, the Hierophant, reversed, is in the position connected with Eleanor's time. By reading the cards' meanings, and using these connections, she could easily pick out the important aspects of the reading.

Interpretation.   Maude, signified by the Lovers card, is making choices about love and learning how to have satisfying relationships. Family, friends, and work relationships are important to her. She needs to be cautious about letting her emotions run away with her, and to make choices for the best of all concerned. Balance is an essential part of any relationship for her.

An important influence is the 6 of Cups in her energy position, indicating that Maude is sharing her gifts and talents. The opposite card, Eleanor's energy, is the 10 of Cups reversed. It depicts a desire for home and family harmony, and also may refer to frustrations or delays around work.

Also of concern is the other Major Arcana card, the Hierophant reversed. The Hierophant indicates conformity, authority, established structures. Reversed, it suggests that nontraditional life choices affect Eleanor's time. Is she trying too hard to conform in some way that isn't true to herself, trying to be a "wife" even though her partner is also female? The opposite card for Maude is the Knight of Swords, indicating a romantic, impulsive nature, skilled in conquering obstacles. Maude is good at her job and values the chance to be the "knight in shining armor" to Eleanor, but is not paying close attention to the consequences to herself.

Next, Maude looks at matches to the true situation, the 7 of Pentacles. There are no other sevens, but there are two other pentacle cards, both in the resource position. The suit of pentacles is connected directly with money and material things, reinforcing the idea that Maude and Eleanor's issues may have more to do with money than they are willing to admit.

Interpretation.   The true situation connects directly with the partner's resources. The 7 of Pentacles indicates the true situation, or the hidden agenda. There is an excellent foundation, and much hard work has been rewarded. In the card image, one pentacle has not yet been added to the pile, so there is still some work to be done. Both Maude's and Eleanor's resources cards are reversed, indicating that they both have issues around scarcity of money and other material things. Eleanor's reversed 8 of Pentacles indicates that things at work are at a standstill. The tools she needs are not available to her, and she is frustrated, echoing the reversed 10 of Cups in her Energy position.

Maude's reversed 2 of Pentacles suggests she is trying to juggle too much, to be everything to everyone—or, in this case, to her partner. The advice is to focus and marshal resources. This could also indicate that Maude is not using her time and resources wisely regarding her work.

Maude's reading helped clarify the issues she noted in the first exercise. Looking at the two reversed resources cards, it occurred to her that she and Eleanor were both highly focused on their home because they both felt they had made sacrifices for it. She decided it might be time to focus on enjoying the home instead of worrying about it. She reaffirmed that Eleanor was trying to help, not harm. She also uncovered an interesting notion about Eleanor's issues around conformity.

After realizing how much she'd been holding back from Eleanor, Maude apologized for her outburst and sat down for a long talk about her work frustrations, once more affirming her strong love and desire to be home with her partner. Maude didn't ask Eleanor to do anything more than listen: "You know, Eleanor, just because I pay more of the bills doesn't mean you have to sacrifice your time to try to make things even. You make our home better just by being here," she said. "I just need to appreciate that more." Eleanor turned to face her partner. "Thank you," she said with emphasis, for this acceptance was something she hadn't been able to give herself.

Knowing that spirituality was one area of life where Maude could truly feel free of the pressure to win and achieve, Eleanor suggested they work on a spell together, to cleanse their home of negative energy. Maude loved the idea, and she made a key suggestion: Their spell (which you can find in the appendix) empowered the gold sofa pillows as carriers of the positive qualities they wanted their home to have.

Jane Speaks

The first step in creating a relationship of equals is communicating—talking and listening. If these two hadn't been able to talk about what was really behind Maude's emotional response to the sofa pillows—if she and Eleanor had just "made up" and moved on—the resentments caused by this fight might fester and eventually spoil their relationship.

I learned this firsthand when I was younger and was living with a boyfriend who decided to go back to college. I was happy to support him by taking over most of the bills and by offering encouragement and help with his schoolwork. To balance my greater financial contribution, we arranged that he would do more housework.

What we didn't spell out as part of this negotiation was that I needed him to continue being a boyfriend—to spend some of his free time with me, to act loving and affectionate toward me, to participate in social life together. Stressed out by college and family problems, he stopped devoting time to "us." I tried for many months to give him space to settle into his new life, but he just withdrew further into solitude and anxiety. When I questioned our relationship and finally ended it, he felt resentful. After all, the floors were still clean!

I'm not sure this partnership could have been saved (and I think we're both much happier being married to other people), but it would have helped if I'd had the knowledge and courage to start a conversation when the problem first arose. I thought I was being noble and doing the right thing by keeping quiet for as long as I could. Instead, by letting resentment build up inside me, I made things a lot more painful than they had to be.

THE GETAWAY WEEKEND

In this all-too-common dilemma, the partners' sexual needs are part of an equals imbalance.

Vicki, forty, a dress shop owner, and George, thirty-eight, a computer programmer, had been married for almost ten years and had two children, Tim and Sophy. They were committed Wiccans and had been active in a coven before job and family responsibilities took up too much time for them to participate.

Those responsibilities made it difficult to schedule "couple time," too. After a particularly busy season, they made plans to take a weekend off, just the two of them. They sent the kids to Grandpa's and took advantage of a getaway weekend deal at a nice resort. George left his pager and cell phone at home, and Vicki scrambled to get the housework done before they left.

They arrived on Saturday morning, spent time by the pool, did some shopping, and had a great dinner where they discussed doing a ritual together to strengthen their relationship, a technique that had been helpful to them in the past. Vicki went to the hot tub to relax some more, still feeling weary and achy from that long burst of housecleaning. George went to the room to set up candles and get out their ritual robes. An hour and a half later, Vicki came in. She headed straight for the bathroom, emerging in her robes after a scented herbal bath. During meditation to draw down the Goddess and the God, George had no problem feeling the energy of the Horned One, and wanted to make love. Vicki, however, fell asleep and began snoring.

What had happened? When George and Vicki met, they loved doing ritual together, especially sexual magic. Over the years, the pressures of a growing family and careers reduced the time and energy available.

George wanted to do a ritual as a part of the weekend because he sensed Vicki missed the regular time to practice their faith together. He saw himself as making an extra effort to provide a context in which they could both enjoy themselves. He had no interest in forcing anything on Vicki, but one of the things that he loved about Wicca was the notion that pleasure is sacred. He felt pressure to reconnect with Vicki on many levels, including the sexual. He had blamed himself for their less-than-full sex life, and this was a chance to make up for his recent preoccupation with work.

Vicki agreed that the freedom Wicca offers around sexual pleasure was important to her. But sex was only a small part of the overall relationship. She sensed that George needed to relax, and she knew raising in energy in ritual was good for them both.

It was very important to her that she feel free to choose. This gained poignancy for her recently: Their daughter had just turned seven, the age at which Vicki had been molested by her older brother. While she felt she had gotten over the abuse, seeing her daughter's innocence had brought back some of Vicki's grief for the parts of childhood she had missed.

One of their misunderstandings had to do with sexuality and sensuality. Sexuality has a goal: getting to second base, raising power, orgasm. It is often about *doing* something. Sensuality is often without a goal: taking in sights, sounds, and smells, enjoying the energy flow, touching and being touched. It is about *being or experiencing* something. Both are important. They look a lot alike, and sensuality often leads to sexuality. It was not unreasonable to assume that this getaway weekend could encompass both.

Like Maude and Eleanor, this couple had discussed the big stuff: whether or not to have children, how to balance careers, and even their getaway weekend. Vicki and George would agree that they wanted to honor each other, that coerced sex was nothing either of them wanted, and that they did need time for themselves as a couple. The differences lay beneath the surface.

Frustrated in more ways than one, George came home from the weekend anxious and unhappy. He knew what the obvious problem was, but he couldn't figure out how to express it to Vicki. He knew there had to be some issue lying beneath it, but he didn't know what that might be. Notice the themes that emerge from his answers to the Clarifying Questions—themes that go far beyond just a problem of sexual desire.

Describe the situation in words. "I've been spending a lot of time at work, and I know that I haven't been as attentive as I could be to Vicki. We went away for a weekend and I did a whole lot to make sure she knew I loved her and wanted to be with her. I even took care of setting up the room for ritual. It seemed like things were going okay, but she fell asleep during our meditation. Afterward, she said she wasn't really interested in having sex with me because it felt like it was a setup to get her into bed. Well, it was in a way. Sex is really important to me, and I thought it was to her. I know it takes time to get in the mood, especially with the stress of the kids and the house and her job and my job. But my needs are important, too!"

Who is involved? "Me, Vicki. Maybe the kids and the job people in a lesser way."

What is happening?   "Our sex life is nonexistent."

Where is this happening?   "Nowhere."

When does this happen?   "Any time I want to make love, Vicki falls asleep, feels sick, or doesn't want to."

How does this happen?   "Sometimes she gets busy with something else, or says 'I'm not there now' or she just ignores the signals. Sometimes she starts an argument."

Why does this happen?   "I guess some of it is stress, and sometimes she does feel bad, and I know we don't have a lot of time. When we first got together, she was working on what her brother did to her, but I think she got over that."

What do I want?   "I want to make love with my wife at least a couple of times a week."

If I could wave my magic wand, what would happen?   "Vicki would be loving and interested, like she was when we first were handfasted. And we'd win the lottery."

What would I do?   "I'd find a way to let Vicki know I love her, and that I express that sexually. I'd spend less energy on the job, so I could be at home more."

What would others do?   "Vicki would understand what I need, and that if she were truthful, she'd see that she needs regular sex, too. The kids would go to sleep on time and stay in their own beds."

How would the situation change?   "Vicki and I would be happy like we used to be."

What is the very best thing that could possibly happen here?   "We'd start having regular, good, happy sex."

What do I think?   "I think Vicki is spending too much time at work and her family is giving her grief."

What is my opinion?   "I believe that if we don't get this straightened out, I'm going to have to consider other options. I don't think this is all my fault."

Who is right?   "I am! And, of course, so is Vicki."

Who is wrong?   "Her family. And she used to be really loving, and liked sex as much as I did. We promised each other that we'd always stay close and not get like other couples who made love once a month."

What do I think is likely in this situation?   "I think things have got to change."

What has happened like this in the past?   "The girl I dated before Vicki cut me off. She said it was because she had to 'find herself,' but I think she was seeing someone else. I thought Vicki had already found herself."

What do I feel? What are my emotions?   "I feel horny. I feel mad that things that used to be good have changed. I feel confused by not knowing what is really happening. I feel worried that our marriage might be in trouble. I'm scared that she might be seeing someone else. I feel really bad about the time I haven't given to our relationship."

What do I need?   "I don't know. I know I can't go on like this: I feel like I'm a stranger and that sometimes I scare Vicki. I guess, at the very bottom, I need to be able to be who I really am, and that includes my physical needs. I need to be connected to my kids. And I think I want to keep my marriage together."

What is the worst thing that could happen and how would it affect me?   "I think the worst thing would be if Vicki were cheating on me. I'd be devastated, like I had been living a lie. And I'd worry about getting AIDS. She would be betraying me. It would mean I had failed."

What are the things I have control over?   "I feel like I don't have any control at all. I guess I can change how much time I spend with Vicki, and how I act around her. I could also ask her point-blank if she is seeing anyone and then deal with that."

What are the things I don't have control over?   "I can't control Vicki, and I can't control the past."

What reality has to shift for my intention to be manifest?   "We would have to get closer again, and she would have to be more accepting, more willing to meet my needs."

How can I bring that about through correspondences? "I could begin to send energy to her and to me, so that we would have more time for one another. I could try to balance my work better so I can bring my full attention to Vicki, and to Tim and Sophy, too. I could look at some simple stuff like phone calls to remind Vicki that I love her. I could work with my patron goddess Athena for more wisdom on how to handle this situation."

Through the questions, George put into words his fear that Vicki was cheating on him, a fear that might be a reflection of pain from an old relationship. He was worried about her family's influence on her, and he felt guilty for not spending enough time with her. He also reaffirmed that he could do some things to bring about change: spending more time at home, making simple loving gestures such as phone calls, asking divine help to get through this difficulty.

As a starting point in this work, he tried the Equals Tarot Spread, which made it clear that this wasn't a problem he could ignore.

Here, the Self is the Major Arcana Card XIII Death, reversed. There are no other cards for the number thirteen.

Interpretation. George is stagnant, frustrated, and without a plan. He is in a stalemate. He feels discouraged and sees unpleasant changes that he cannot control. Tension mounts, and there is no easy way out of the problem.

In this reading, the Self card is one of the Major Arcana, so all other cards in this category are read next, beginning with the next highest number. The cards that are exactly opposite these cards are then read as secondary influences. Thus the Star, XVII, representing Vicki's resources, is read with a secondary influence of the opposite, the 7 of Cups.

Interpretation. George needs to take special note that Vicki's resources, represented by the Star reversed, are strained.

The future seems bleak, and one of her most important resources, hope, is not available. Material things may indeed be a part of the problem. George's resource card, the 7 of Cups, indicates he may be having some problems also, preferring fantasy or illusion to reality. In this card of too many choices, the cups are hidden by clouds, indicating that an unspoken problem may be hurting the equitable distribution of resources.

Next V, the Hierophant, representing George's time, is read with a secondary influence of the opposite, Vicki's time, 4 of Cups (reversed).

Interpretation.   George's time, represented by the Hierophant, brings up the possibility that he has authority or responsibility issues around his use of time. This might be coming from either his career or from his family, but the card indicates he is struggling with how he can use his time in an acceptable way. Vicki's time, represented by the 4 of Cups (reversed), indicates she is moving away from complacency toward a new order of living.

Next, VII, the Chariot, Vicki's energy, is read, with a secondary influence of the opposite, George's energy, XII, the Hanged Man.

Interpretation.   Vicki's energy, represented by the Chariot, is considerate and kind, but she can be too focused on maintaining control. George's energy, indicated by the Hanged Man, indicates changes. There is an emphasis on leaving the past behind and moving into a new spiritual depth. George is entering a testing period. Vicki may need to gather her strength and decide on a goal.

Next, XII, the Hanged Man, George's energy is read with a secondary influence of the opposite, Vicki's energy, VII, the Chariot. The meanings are the same as the reading above, with the double reading indicating this is a very important aspect of the situation.

The True Situation is the 9 of Pentacles, reversed. There are no other nines or pentacles.

Interpretation.   This situation is insecure. It is possible that they will lose all they have achieved.

Because of the large number of Major Arcana cards, this is a reading about a very significant situation. It directly addresses what is going on for George and Vicki, and it points out some places where misunderstandings are likely.

Having discovered what at least some of his part of the problem was, George looked at what he could fix. First, he looked his fear in the face. Fear of the unknown saps our time, our energy, and our resources in defending against imagined threats. His greatest fear was that Vicki had a new lover. He asked her if she was seeing someone else, knowing this might or might not open a discussion about their sex life. His goal was not so much to fix their sex life as to deal with his own fears.

Vicki, interrupted while putting away laundry, was surprised that he would ask, and with a rather baffled expression, said no, there was no one else. "Why do you ask?" He told her that he was feeling distant from her, a feeling that seemed to echo a pattern from his old relationship. She turned back to sorting socks without taking the conversation further.

Still, George had gotten his answer. He knew her to be a truthful person, and even with his anxiety about this issue he could not help but believe her.

Once he had dealt with the fear, George still had some work to do. While answering the Clarifying Questions, he had made a list of things he could change within himself and about his actions. He set out to act more positively, whether Vicki chose to do anything or not. He took a hard look at his own use of time, energy, and material resources, and he looked for ways to allocate more for his relationship. For him, this included apologizing for past unhelpful behavior, managing his work responsibilities to allow more family time, and being more conscious of how he behaved around Vicki.

This last goal, George knew, would be the most difficult. He didn't know what Vicki was feeling or thinking. It seemed she experienced his advances as pressure to perform, rather than expressions of love. George knew his own sexual feelings were not bad or wrong, and he acknowledged that the current situation was frustrating. His own work right now was not to take out that frustration on his partner. George realized that he could give Vicki more space and freedom, and he could express affection and sensuality without expecting gratification as a result.

George valued knowledge and wisdom, and he had developed a special affinity for the Greek goddess Athena. He performed the Talisman Spell (see appendix) to empower a little topaz-eyed figurine of an owl as a symbol of his connection to Athena, goddess of wisdom. George did not ask for Vicki to become more sexual with him. Instead, he asked for wisdom to be a better husband, to learn and grow as a man and a father, and to manage his own desires so that they did not hurt his wife. He put the little owl on the nightstand next to his side of the bed, to remind him that he could invoke Athena's aid in being a better husband to Vicki.

Cleaning Up Your Side of the Street

If you are in a situation where equality is an issue, you may think you already understand the problem. The message of this chapter is that before you try to negotiate a more equal partnership, it's vital to do the work of honestly exploring your own feelings, fears, and experiences. Maude and George, through simple exercises, each gained a better understanding of the situations that troubled them, and some ideas about their partners' perspective. They also came to realize how their feelings fed on past experiences—experiences that might have little to do with current situations—and how they might act now to improve things.

The work they did was not a solution, but a start. The East is about beginnings and communication. The first person you need to hear is yourself.

If we believe we are truly equals in our relationship, we don't wait for the other person to change. We clean up our side of the street. If we both live in a house and you are not home when the pipe bursts, I don't wait for you to get home, discuss it with you, and get your input. I turn off the water, mop up the mess, and salvage what I can. I trust that if I do the next good thing (i.e., turn off the water), our relationship supports it. Likewise, if you see areas you can work on, start those improvements now.

Cynthia Speaks

My husband Chris took two years to die of metastatic cancer of the tongue. During the acute stages of Chris's cancer, this notion of "equals" was very difficult for me. It was much easier for me to put his needs first and ignore my own. He was the one who was dying. He was the one being fed through a tube. He was the one with immediate, urgent physical needs. He had a limited time on this earth to enjoy the pleasures of the body, and my time with him was short. His emotional resources were small. Many people who loved him wanted to be with him.

The temptation was to live our lives completely focused on Chris and his cancer. Because I felt the scarcity of his resources, energy, and time so acutely, I found myself wanting to give him as much of mine as I could. His family, society in general, the medical personnel, his children, our Wiccan friends, and even my own training and personality overtly and subtly encouraged me to devalue my needs because of the urgency of his. It did not take long for me to need some way to make the notion of equals practical.

I suspect that I did not do a great job of staying in touch with my own needs and wants, thoughts, and feelings. The truth was that his needs were more urgent, and his resources, time, and energy were more limited. But I did—with Chris's encouragement and support—honor some of my needs.

I received a great deal of criticism when I was adamant about having time and space to myself. I knew that I could not spend twenty-four hours a day, seven days a week, with Chris and cancer.

Together, Chris and I decided that it was important to be equals, despite the disparity of our circumstances and roles. One way to honor that decision was to have time for myself, doing something I enjoyed, and sticking with it except in a life-and-death medical crisis. So on Wednesday night I taught a class on Wicca for an hour and then went out with the class for dinner. On Sunday I met friends at a coffee shop to gossip and talk about art and writing.

Sometimes coven members came to stay with Chris, occasionally family members or friends. But someone had to be there, and whenever that someone wasn't me, I had to make the arrangements. I learned a great deal about the notion of equals, not only between the two of us, but also in terms of relationships with others. I learned that I needed a backup plan for when people failed to arrive on time. I learned about communication and commitment, resentment and gratitude. I found myself evaluating my need for a break as more important and urgent than the needs of the people around me. Somehow I felt they (especially his family) "owed" me, and should be extra respectful of my needs. With time and perspective, I now see that each of us was grieving in our own way, and that each grief was equally important and urgent.

The Message of the East

When working to build or improve a relationship, the first step is knowing yourself.

- Take time to observe situations in which you feel you are giving or taking an unequal amount of time, energy, or material resources.

- Do some structured thinking to determine what your real feelings are, and what might have caused you to feel that way.
- Use tools such as the Clarifying Questions and the Equals Tarot Spread to help you focus on the forces at work.
- Take positive action. Without trying to change anyone else's behavior, do whatever you can to behave in an equal and helpful way in your relationship. This includes seeking divine help in whatever way is meaningful for you.

Even working alone, there are actions you can take to make things better. By taking those actions, you invoke the energies you will need as you engage with your partner to make things better. Those energies are yours—your best wisdom, generosity, and love.

Making Decisions Together

The Principle of Consensus

As we saw in chapter 1, a healthy relationship starts with understanding your own feelings, concerns, and experiences. In this chapter, we'll discuss ways to build on that understanding by working with your partner, setting goals for your relationship, and taking action toward achieving them.

The goals you achieve don't have to be Olympic feats. You set them by discovering things you want to do together and making your shared goals a priority for each of you. When consensus is truly in place, both in words and in actions, both you and your partnership will grow stronger. The energies of the South (associated in various traditions with fire, passion, summer, and the power of will) operate as a forge, melding distinct individuals into a strong whole.

For some Pagans, drawn to this spiritual path by its strong emphasis on independence of thought and action, this Principle of Consensus may be difficult to put into practice. Without consensus, individuals in partnerships can slide away from truly relating to one another, and will merely coexist. This chapter will also explore ideas for accepting consensus and bringing it to life in your relationships.

> **We choose our path together.** We both agree on choices that are for both of us, and when we do not agree, we do not follow that path until we are in agreement. We commit to discussing and wrestling with our hopes and fears, wants and needs, money, power, sexuality. We don't try to manipulate each other.

If I want to move to Michigan, I don't start looking for jobs there unless I've talked with you and gotten your full agreement—not "oh, okay, whatever" but a freely given approval, offered with a real understanding of what it will mean for everyone concerned.

Consensus is based on honor, on being trustworthy. It requires listening to our partners and ourselves, being willing to try new ideas, taking responsibility for our own stuff, and doing the things we say we will do. When a healthy consensus is in place, each person in the relationship gets most of his or her needs and wants met. Consensus is about having the right to choose, to say yes or no or something else. It is not about winning, dominating, or intimidating.

Myth: The Bull Fight

The following couple's lack of consensus about the fundamentals of their marriage literally led them to war.

In Irish mythology, Medb and Ailill were a "power couple"—each of royal lineage with plenty of wealth, livestock, troops, and household goods. One day, Ailill snuggled up to his wife in bed and said something like, "You know, I've been thinking. You are *so* much better off since you married me."

These were fighting words. Irish law at the time granted greater privileges to the party who had brought more property to a marriage, and if Medb were not as wealthy as Ailill, her position would have been subservient.

Furious at the implications of his words, she jumped up and insisted on pulling out every household object, comparing their linens, counting every cow and sheep. When their riches were added up, she and her husband were absolutely even except for one thing: a spectacular white-horned bull. The bull was Ailill's, though it had formerly belonged to Medb. (The medieval chronicler tells us the bull had changed hands of its own accord, because it didn't want to be owned by a woman!)

To even up the score, Medb sought out another bull, equally beautiful and strong. It belonged to someone else, so she started a great war to try to capture it. She lost hundreds of warriors, and both bulls ended up dead.

If these two had been able to agree not to compete, to work together to protect and support their people, a lot of brave Irish lives would have been spared. It probably wasn't much consolation that the Cattle-Raid of Cuialnge inspired some of Ireland's greatest poetry.

A PACT BETWEEN EQUALS

Before we go on, it's important to know that in some circumstances consensus is impossible.

Consensus cannot be reached except between equals. If you and a partner begin to work on building consensus, but keep running into problems, it may be a good idea to reassess the equality in your relationship.

Some relationships are not run by consensus. For example, some Wiccan and Pagan groups choose to govern themselves by a system of hierarchy. This is perfectly acceptable, as long as no one is pretending to be governing by consensus. Other nonconsensual relationships include that of a teacher and student, a healer and patient, or a parent and child (until the child has reached adulthood).

Consensus cannot be reached unless both partners are willing and able to be honorable and trustworthy over time.   The stresses of modern life—social, personal, environmental, physical—bring about many emotional and mental disorders that can be successfully treated and that do not get in the way of being trustworthy. For example, medication and talk therapy can often ease clinical depression or post-traumatic stress. People with these illnesses, no matter where they are on the continuum, are able to be trustworthy and respectful to the extent that they are realistic in their expectations of themselves and others.

Other people—active alcohol and drug abusers, the domestically violent, sexual and/or emotional abusers, profoundly codependent people, and those with chronic untreated personality disorders—are simply not capable of this. Their basic drives are not toward partnership, but toward self-absorption or self-destruction. Such people are out of touch with our consensual reality or are not able to interact ethically within our social context.

These same people may be able to keep their word for a day, a week, a month, a year, but at some point they *will* go back to their diseases. They will probably deny this is so, at the time of the discussion. In the end, though, their own needs and fears will be served at the expense of anyone or anything that gets in their way. When they do break their word, they may blame the failure on their partners' actions or attitudes. At the other extreme, they might absolve partners of all responsibility, playing the martyr, thus robbing their partners of the chance to learn about their own rights and responsibilities.

It is a different case when one party in a relationship is truly committed to a recovery process. Such people will make mistakes, but they will be doing their best and succeeding more often as their work progresses. They will be open to correcting what is wrong, no matter what is required. They will make amends and learn from any problem that arises.

The key difference between the two types of people is this: Active addicts and abusers will insist on protecting their supply or prerogatives or delusions. Those who are capable of putting their relationship ahead of those things are candidates for consensus.

We value trustworthiness and honor in friends, families, and ourselves. While no one is perfect, it seems that whenever trust and honor are consistently absent, relationships get broken and there is no room for love, much less consensus.

An example: Simple things are important in building honor and trust.

Debbie left her car to be repaired, and it was supposed to be ready Tuesday. Things got backed up at the shop, and they told her it would be ready Wednesday. The service department said they would call to let her know when it would be done. By midafternoon Wednesday Debbie had called three times, but no one could tell her when to expect her car.

By Thursday morning, she was talking to the owner of the dealership. She got what she wanted—an apology and a loaner car until they finished the work. Yet she had spent a day in uncertainty and anger, wasting time when she could have been using her vehicle. The shop did not do what they said they would do until she held them accountable.

She thought she and the dealer had reached consensus about something that concerned both of them: her car repair and their payment. It then became clear that they had not. The apology and the loaner car were the dealership's way of making amends. Now, if she chooses to do business with these people, she obtains in writing what they agree to do and how they will make amends if they fail.

Trustworthy people do what they say they will do when they say they will do it. People who don't do this are lacking in the basics of consensus, and the people around them are wise to be wary.

A positive example: Gene was a senior in high school. He had changed schools after his freshman year, leaving his best friends behind. In protest, or because of genuine academic trouble, his sophomore grades had gone from respectable to dreadful. His junior year saw improvement, and his senior year—well, he made honor roll the first four grading periods and was admitted to college. For this fifth grading period he could have done just about nothing and still have had both diploma and college admission. Yet he brought home the best average he had ever had!

Trustworthy people do what they agree they'll do, even if the words are not in a contract. They try to live by the spirit, not just the letter. And they do what they *need* to do before they do what they *want* to do. In Gene's case, by earning a high school diploma and agreeing to go to college, he "agreed" to continue learning and did so to the best of his ability. He might have preferred to be out with friends rather than scrambling to get schoolwork done. But as a trustworthy person, he did his work first.

It seems our most painful experiences are betrayals of trust, and yet it is very easy in our hectic lives to let honor slide, to put it aside for the needs of the moment. The promise to ourselves not to say yes to another ritual this month doesn't seem nearly as important as the request for healing made in heartfelt need. The promise to take a child to the movies today doesn't seem as important as the crisis at work. Two lonely people may break their marriage promises rather than confront their spouses about being unhappy.

Honorable people make commitments only when they are reasonably sure of being able to keep them. Each person in the above examples may truly have intended to keep his or her word, but circumstances changed. The healing was so urgently needed. Handling the work crisis would build one's chances for promotion. The two people were at the same big convention, and it seemed so comforting to run into a friendly colleague. Typically, they didn't see their actions as betrayals at the time, as harmful to themselves and others. Yet their dishonorable actions did harm them, and the people closest to them, as well.

The unspoken promises we make, or that our society makes for us, complicate our trust relationships. When we become parents, we don't take a formal vow to feed, clothe, shelter, love, and nurture our children. Yet we have no trouble understanding that the parent who leaves a three-year-old alone is not trustworthy.

A betrayal of trust harms not only the betrayed but also the betrayer. The wounds are deep within, and they do not heal unless they are recognized and cleansed. Here we begin to ask ourselves what we are really trying to accomplish and why we betrayed our word, spoken or unspoken.

Being trustworthy requires constant attention, though it seems to get easier with practice. When situations seem to force our choices, trustworthy people consider the consequences of their actions before they take them. They will take responsibility for their choices, without blaming others. If they cannot do what they say they will do, if they harm themselves or others, they communicate with those who are affected and make amends promptly.

Consensus cannot be reached when one partner is responsible for something and the other is not.   If I am caring for my young nephew, you and I cannot reach consensus that I will leave the child while we go get a milkshake. This is not a choice for both of us alone. The boy and his parents are involved. He is my responsibility, not yours. We may come to consensus that we will get the milkshake after my sister comes home and I am no longer responsible for my nephew.

You and I cannot reach consensus that you will not go to work today. That is your responsibility, not mine. It can be very tempting to spread the responsibility around, but that is not what we mean by consensus. We have the right to choose only when we are willing and able to take responsibility for the consequences.

Consensus cannot be reached when one partner is considerably more powerful than the other, unless the more powerful willingly gives equal power for the decision to the other. The most obvious: No adult can have consensus with a nonadult about sexual relations between them. The adult cannot give the child equal power as an adult, and our laws rightly reflect that.

No one with a gun to my head can achieve consensus with me to take all my money. They might have my agreement, but the element of coercion makes consensus impossible. If I do not also have the same weapon we are not sharing power, and saying no has dire consequences for me. Another: If you hold the power to fire me from my job, we cannot agree in consensus to have a sexual relationship. Your power keeps me from choosing freely.

My young nephew and I may reach a consensus about what game to play or what movie to watch, within parameters that are set by me as the person with more responsibility. I share my power to choose how we spend our time. I may offer him Monopoly, and he may suggest chess. We may compromise on Scrabble, or play all three. I would be exceeding good sense, as well as my authority, to agree to play "Let's Run into the Busy Street."

Responsible parents and caretakers do not allow children and teenagers to use consensus in making decisions when the young people's safety and well-being are at stake. At the same time, as young people grow up, such parents do give them the opportunity to practice making consensus-based decisions in appropriate areas.

Cycles of Consensus

We breathe in and out and in. The seasons change from warm to cold. The waves approach the shore, then retreat, then approach. This is the rhythm of life, of change.

Relationships, too, follow a predictable, undulating cycle. Things go along peacefully, even pleasantly, for a time. Something happens to change or complicate the situation. We respond to the change or complications, coming to some sort of compromise. Once the situation is resolved, we have another period of rest before things change or complicate the situation again. This is a natural, normal, appropriate cycle, as ordinary as night and day. It is simply the way life is.

There are three basic ways the cycle can function. The differences are in the way partners handle changes or complications.

CYCLE OF HURT AND MANIPULATION

The first way—responding to change by hurting or manipulating others—is unhealthy and can never lead to consensus. Here's an example:

Oliver has a problem with his temper. Often he goes for a time without an outburst. Then small things begin to build, and he becomes testier. His partner Malcolm doesn't want to rock the boat, so he smooths it all over and tries to keep the peace. Eventually, a week or a month later, something happens—at work, at home, or in traffic—that sends Oliver into a rage. He yells, screams, throws things, or shoves Malcolm. These are his ways of dealing with changes and complications.

After Oliver "gets it all out," he's very sorry. He promises he'll never do it again. He may even bring home flowers, do a rededication ritual with Malcolm, or give him extra attention. Things are so much quieter and peaceful. Who would want to have the honeymoon end? But tensions begin to build—and the same thing will happen again.

Malcolm was planning a special party for his best friends from college, who were coming to town for the weekend. But Malcolm knew that eventually Oliver would blow up, because he always did. So during the early part of the week, Malcolm unconsciously began to needle his partner. By Saturday, Oliver had already gone through his outburst, and he was extra charming to Malcolm's friends as a way of making amends. The party went off without a hitch.

The honeymoon period is not a consensus. It is only a part of a cycle of violence and denial. Remember that consensus cannot be reached unless both partners are willing and able to be honorable and trustworthy over time. Oliver was not doing his part to deal with his temper, nor was Malcolm doing his part to deal with his own role in the situation.

Consensus cannot be reached when one partner is responsible for something and the other is not. By trying to manage and control his partner's temper, Malcolm was taking away Oliver's responsibility for himself. Consensus cannot be reached when one partner is considerably more powerful than the other. Oliver's displays of temper were threatening and threw off the balance of power between him and his partner.

A HEALTHIER WAY: PLANNING FOR CYCLES

The second way of dealing with cycles is to anticipate changes and complications, and make some decisions ahead of time. When an anticipated situation occurs, we know what to do in line with consensus.

A simple example: Our group plans to hold the Summer Solstice ritual at the rose garden in the park, but we agree that if it is rainy and the ground is wet, we will hold the ritual under the shelter.

Making plans to anticipate changes in a relationship—What will happen if I change jobs? How will we stay connected after the baby comes?—can be a valuable way to better understand each other's goals and priorities. In the early stages of a relationship, partners often look for signs that the other person is including the relationship in plans for the future. The next step is actually making plans together.

NEGOTIATING CONSENSUS

The third way to deal with cycles of change is based on a negotiation model. A common analogy is the negotiation of a labor contract. Workers and management come to the table as equals if they each believe the other is necessary to the relationship. Likewise it's important that partners in a relationship build consensus from a foundation of equality. A successful consensus negotiation, like a labor contract or a peace treaty, follows a few standard steps:

The two parties involved have a common goal. Often a part of the process is to define the goal in a way that both partners can accept. A company and a union may affirm that they want to produce quality products at reasonable prices. A boyfriend and girlfriend may both believe that their relationship is important and worth preserving.

The people involved recognize that something has changed, or is about to change, and that it needs to be discussed. Even if one side is okay with how things are, it is time to at least discuss the future. For the cycle described earlier, this is where the situation changes and complicates matters.

At this stage, the parties may make lists of things they want. A union might want higher wages, a new lunchroom, and seniority guarantees. A girlfriend might want fewer dust bunnies under the bed, less late-night computer gaming, and a proposal of marriage within six months.

In each case, the opposite side has its own list. The company might want a longer workweek, fewer holidays, and the freedom to move the plant elsewhere. The boyfriend might want a neater bathroom, help in meeting his goal of going to graduate school, and no discussion of marriage for at least two years.

Despite their common goal, the particulars are going to be a problem. Let's assume they are willing and able to discuss things reasonably:

They choose an appropriate time and place to begin the discussion, and schedule times to meet for additional discussion. They do not expect to ambush each other, using time pressure as coercion to force agreement. They choose a time when both sides can be free from outside distractions (for instance, no phones or pagers beeping) and a place that is not emotionally loaded, away from the usual places where they interact. They know it will take some time, so they set up other meetings, perhaps with a restricted agenda or specific time frame.

The next step is pretty obvious: *They specifically define what changes or complications are being discussed.* It is easy to fantasize wrongly, and that leads to misunderstandings and problems. Especially when there is tension over a change or complication, it is easy to believe one is taking the reasonable and logical stance and the other the unreasonable and illogical one.

So it's important to talk clearly about the details: Does the union want an additional dollar per hour over a five-year contract, or two dollars an hour over a one-year contract? Does the girlfriend want her partner off the computer by nine every night, or by midnight on weeknights?

With the issues defined, it's clear that neither side will get everything it wants.

Set your own priorities. Which issue is the most important for you? In our example, let's say the union is especially interested in the seniority issues, and the company is especially interested in moving to the next county. The girlfriend is especially interested in marriage, and the boyfriend in graduate school.

Sometimes just getting the specifics on the table can bring easy compromises. Knowing the company wants to move, but to retain its skilled labor force, can help the union gain incentives for trained workers. Knowing her boyfriend wants to get an advanced degree may bolster his girlfriend's case for healthier sleep patterns.

Here is where the analogy breaks down. In a labor negotiation, it is wise to withhold information, to give away as little as possible. In a relationship built on consensus, we want to be as open and honest as we can be with our partners and ourselves, not making a game or competition of the discussion. In the cycle, this is where the compromise begins.

A consensus negotiation is successful when the participants develop creative solutions that satisfy, and perhaps more than satisfy, all partners.

Home or Away?

In the following story, the partners had already made some plans, and they now had to deal with a change that they hadn't expected.

Marie and Richard, in their late twenties, had been living together for two years. They followed a Celtic path in their Wiccan practice, and they spent time together exploring the history of Ireland and crafting rituals to honor the ancient gods of that country. On a more practical level, they had begun saving to buy a house together. This was especially important to Marie, whose family valued real estate ownership as a sign of adulthood.

In the same week, they got two pieces of good news: Richard received an unexpected tax refund, and Marie received a cash settlement from an old employer who was found guilty of unfair practices.

Richard was thrilled. Finally they could go to Ireland! He did some research and found a great deal on a trip that would take them to many of the places they most wanted to see. When he showed the information to Marie, she stared at him blankly. "You mean you don't want to put that money toward the house?"

They looked at each other in confusion. Neither of them liked to fight, and serious disagreements between them were rare. At the same moment, they both gave in. "Okay, you're right, we should save it for the house," conceded Richard just as Marie said, "No, no, let's go if you want to."

What to do? They both cared a great deal about both goals. The trip was something they'd talked about as a way to deepen their knowledge and their spiritual bond to each other. The house was a concrete goal that made sense financially and would also benefit their spiritual life by giving them a more private place to meditate and worship. The money was not enough to actually buy a house, though it would make a significant dent in the amount they needed to save. The trip and incidental expenses would use up all the unexpected money, with nothing left over for the house fund.

The premade decisions—their shared spiritual path and the choice to save for a house—were helpful, narrowing the options down to two. That still left them with a choice to make.

They decided to visit a pond near their house, where they often went to talk things over or enjoy the cycles of nature. They brought a copy of the Consensus Questions (see appendix) and sat down under a tree. Marie led Richard through the questions, asking without interrupting or commenting, giving him plenty of time to answer each one aloud.

What do you really want? What is most important? "I really want to enjoy our life together. What is most important to me is that we keep the good things we have going, going."

What right or rights do you want to exercise? What responsibilities go with them? "I'd like the right to spend money that I didn't expect on something fun. As long as I don't hurt anyone, I don't see any responsibilities—as long as I make sure the necessities are covered."

What kinds of pressure are you feeling? From whom? What does your partner seem to want? "I'm feeling some pressure to make a quick decision: The special on the Ireland trip will only be available through Saturday. I'm also feeling some of the 'do the responsible thing and save for the house,' and that is mostly from your family, through you. I'm feeling some pressure not to give in to the 'sensible' thing, and I'm feeling some pressure to get away from the everyday grind. You seem to want this, too, but I think you're also too caught up in your parents' expectations."

What is your bottom line? Is this worth your while? "The bottom line is that I'll go along with saving for the house if it is really important to you, but I'd really love to take this money and celebrate. I know how I can be; if we don't go, I'll get resentful and start being hypercritical, and that will make things bad. I do love you, so I guess it is worth my while to resolve this."

What kind of time is involved here? Energy? Resources? "Well, if we put it all toward the house, we could start looking for a place five or six months earlier. If we go to Ireland, it will be a ten-day vacation. We didn't put any energy into the money, so we can use it as free resources."

What hasn't worked so far? What have I tried? What were the results? "Assuming that you would see it my way didn't work. I tried to explain it to you, but you still don't agree."

Have other people been in a similar situation? What did they try? Did it work? "My brother and his wife won five thousand dollars in a lottery. They split the money in half. He bought new fishing gear and she started a college fund for the kids. They seemed pretty happy with it."

What approximates what you want? What conditions are present? "I remember last year when you brought that puppy home to surprise me. I was so pleased that you thought of me and my love for dogs, and you loved the puppy, too. But in a couple of days, my allergies kicked up. Medication didn't help, so we had to give the puppy away. We both wanted that puppy a lot, but you wanted me comfortable more than you wanted the puppy. We learned from the experience, and we'll get an outside dog when we buy the house. You didn't get what you wanted, but you really made me feel as if you were considering my needs and didn't take it personally when life got in the way."

What are some options? List at least three that are not mentioned above, including playful ones. "Well, I could go to Ireland on my own with my money. Or I could offer to pay your way so we could go together. Or we could take out a loan for the trip. Or we could start a dog-sitting business to raise the money!"

Next, Richard asked Marie the same things, agreeing not to discuss the answers until both had had a chance to go through the questions.

What do you really want? What is most important? "I really wish to have our own house, but more important, I want us to stay together and be happy."

What right or rights do you want to exercise? What responsibilities go with them? "I want to have some say about how our money is spent. I want to go to Ireland, too, but we would be better off saving. I am being responsible."

What kinds of pressure are you feeling? From whom? What does your partner seem to want? "I'm feeling pressured to say okay to the Ireland trip because it would make you so happy. And me, too. I really want to go. I'm feeling pressured to save because real estate prices are going up, and if we don't get our act together, we'll never be able to afford what we'd like to have. The deal you're looking at has some time constraints, so you're pushing for a decision to go."

What is your bottom line? Is this worth your while? "I'll go to Ireland and have a good time. But I'd really rather save the money."

What kind of time is involved here? Energy? Resources? "I only have three vacation days left this year, so I'd have to take a week without pay. I would have to work extra hours to keep us on our saving schedule. While I think we would really enjoy it, I don't know if our finances are really in as good a shape as you think."

What hasn't worked so far? What have I tried? What were the results? "I tried explaining what we should do and why it was best. You seemed to get it, but you still weren't convinced."

Have other people been in a similar situation? What did they try? Did it work? "Your brother and sister-in-law won some money and they divided it in half. He went out and spent it on himself and she put her half away for a rainy day. She was upset that he blew his half, and I don't blame her. I guess I would feel like you weren't really trying to be serious about the house—and me!—if you insisted on the trip."

What approximates what I want? What conditions are present? "We always have been able to work things out in the past, and we are very open about our finances. Any solution here should continue that pattern."

What are some options? List at least three that are not mentioned above, including playful ones. "We could spend half on another kind of vacation, and we could save half. We could give it away to the animal shelter. We could agree to build a replica of the Blarney Stone in our new house with the money from your taxes!"

This question-and-answer session helped them to understand some of the reasons behind their choices, and it brought out some issues, like Marie's vacation time, that they needed to consider when making up their minds. They decided to take a little time off from the discussion, then to sit down after dinner and draw Tarot cards before trying to reach a decision.

That evening, Richard got out his Tarot deck, which he and Marie had used before when solving problems. Marie put on some quiet music, and they took a few moments of silence to ground and center themselves. Richard pulled the first card, the Chariot, and Marie led him through the One-Card Meditation (see appendix).

His first journey put him in the place of the figure standing in the chariot, and he noticed the catlike beasts pulling it. Richard was reminded of the phrase "herding cats," often used to describe attempts to organize Pagans, and he noticed that the animals didn't seem to be going anywhere.

Next, he focused on the city behind the chariot, reminding him of foreign lands and the places he wanted to go.

On his final meditative entry into the card, Richard noticed a

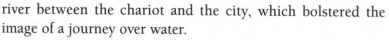

river between the chariot and the city, which bolstered the image of a journey over water.

From this experience he came up with these options, some of which are similar to the ones he described earlier:

1. He could pay for the trip himself (pulling the chariot).
2. He could wait to travel (remaining on his side of the river).
3. He could walk away from his relationship (his chariot) to achieve his goal alone.

While Richard wrote this down, Marie returned his card to the deck and shuffled it thoroughly. To her surprise, she drew—the Chariot! They couldn't help laughing. Then she did the meditation with Richard guiding her.

First, she was drawn to the chariot itself and noticed it was facing away from the city.

Next, she looked at the city and its buildings, and to her they represented the goal of a house.

Finally, Marie connected with the beasts pulling the chariot, and she noticed that one was white and one was black, and that they seemed to be pulling in different directions.

From her experience she generated these options:

1. Agree with good grace on a common goal and turn their relationship (their chariot) toward achieving it.
2. Pull in the same direction, working as a team and using their combined strengths.
3. Find people in the situation who are engaging in black-and-white thinking (such as her relatives who believed so strongly in home ownership), and disengage from those thoughts.
4. Additionally she came up with a practical thought: If they did decide to take the trip, they might achieve some of what she wanted from a house by turning part of their apartment into a meditation space.

Richard and Marie interpreted the drawing of the same card as a sign that their hearts and minds were not that far apart, that their differences didn't run deep. The black-and-white symbolism resonated clearly with Marie, who realized how much her words were parroting her family's thinking instead of expressing her own. She considered for a few minutes: What do I truly want for myself? She wanted a house, to be sure, but it was more important for her to grow spiritually and emotionally with Richard.

With this in mind, Marie was able to agree from her heart that the trip was the best use of their money. Richard was delighted, and he agreed to help her construct their ritual space.

Having made this decision, they still wanted to save for a house. They agreed on some practical steps to get extra money—cutting expenses, volunteering for overtime—then decided to do the Brigid Prosperity Spell (in the appendix).

This prosperity spell helped them focus their spiritual energy on their goal and ask divine help in achieving it.

——————————— *Jane Speaks* ———————————

Of course, you don't have to undertake a high-level negotiation for each decision. My husband and I just spent two minutes making a consensus decision about what to do for lunch. I stated my priority—I'm working on this book and I don't want to take the time to go out or prepare a big meal. He stated his priority—he was hungry but he didn't want to go to the store. We decided to eat something already on hand that could be prepared quickly.

The important point about this negotiation, as with many consensus decisions, is that no one answer is right. He might have decided to go out and get some food he strongly desired, or one of us might not have wanted any lunch at all. The "right" answer is the one that best satisfies all parties. Our quick discussion established what would best satisfy each of us.

Because we're used to making decisions together, we both offered our ideas freely, and each contributed to cooking and cleanup to carry out our decision together. This small decision helped reinforce our pattern of consensus, so we're more likely to follow the same pattern when a bigger problem arises.

And now I'll stop writing for a moment and eat my spaghetti!

Incidents and Patterns

One source of confusion is a lack of understanding about two types of issues, which philosophers call "discrete" and "contiguous." A discrete issue happens at one point in time—Marie and Richard's windfall, for example, or the specific question of Jane's lunch. A contiguous issue is something that extends over time and forms a pattern. In chapter 1, we explored a contiguous issue between George, who desired more sexuality in his relationship, and Vicki, who did not.

Here's another idea from philosophy that applies in many relationships: the "fallacy." Philosophers use that word to describe an idea that sounds logical but isn't true. (A classic: "All mothers are women, therefore all women must be mothers.") When we're thinking in fallacies, we try to describe things in artificial categories, then whine because life doesn't match the categories we've set up. One very common fallacy is confusing discrete and contiguous parts of a relationship.

My offer to bring you a book next Thursday is a discrete offer. If I forget it one time, well, that's not the end of the world. But it may raise a question about my trustworthiness to do what I say I will do when I say I'll do it. If I apologize and do bring the book, then the incident is probably not very important in the larger scheme. If I apologize, promise I'll do it next time, fail to do it, apologize, promise again, and so on, then this discrete offer may have some contiguous aspects. I may be trying to say something covertly about the relationship or about my feelings or about the book. If you ignore it, then we are both missing an opportunity to grow.

Something we've all heard is the complaint "You never say you love me, cherish me, find me attractive, and so forth," and the standard answer "I'm living with you, aren't I? That should be enough!" Clearly, one person is asking for some discrete or point-in-time considerations, and the other person is deliberately using a contiguous or long-term answer to avoid the issue. Even the longest terms need regular reinforcement, reassessment, and rebalancing.

Myth: The Couple in the Cave

This example of a mix-up between discrete and contiguous events is quite literally a classic—it comes from an ancient Roman myth.

Dido was a queen, building her own African city. Aeneas was a son of the goddess Venus, but had fallen on hard times, for he was on the losing side of the Trojan War. He and his men had to flee across storm-tossed seas before landing on the shores of Dido's country.

Venus plotted to throw Dido and Aeneas together, figuring that if the queen loved him, her son and his men would be safe. She arranged to trap the couple together in a cave during a thunderstorm. As you might expect with a plot hatched by the goddess of love, it worked. Dido forgot all about her vow to stay faithful to her dead husband, and Aeneas forgot all about his assignment from Jupiter to build a city in Italy. When the storm was over, the two of them emerged from the cave, adjusting their clothing and smiling blissfully at each other.

Trouble was, they didn't have consensus about what the encounter meant to them. Aeneas was thinking something like, "Hmmm, that was pleasant. I could rest here for a while, no problem." Meanwhile Dido was thinking, "We're married!"

The misunderstanding didn't bother them for a while. They had a great time together. Then Jupiter sent a messenger to remind Aeneas he had to move on to Italy. When the king of the gods spoke, the ancient Romans knew they'd better listen. It was time for Aeneas to go.

Aeneas knew Dido would be upset, and he tried to hide his preparations for leaving. When she found out, Dido berated her lover, saying his departure would take away her "husband." He said something like, "Husband? What husband?"

Because she mistook a pleasant interlude for a lifetime commitment, she wasn't able to let go, to accept her disappointment while remembering the delights they'd enjoyed. Dido grew angry and depressed, and she eventually committed suicide.

THE HAIRCUT

In the days after their getaway weekend (see chapter 1), George had spent a lot of time thinking about his struggle with his own sexual desires and Vicki's lack of interest. George had made a real effort to be loving without pressuring her: He had cut back his work hours to spend more time with the family, and he had done personal rituals to help him become a better husband. After a couple of weeks without change, George decided it was time to talk with her about his feelings and to ask her to work toward resuming their sex life.

He thought he had all the pieces in place. George had chosen a night when the kids had friends over and were safely in the other room watching a movie. He made dinner and cleaned up the kitchen. And after all his effort, it still wasn't the right time. Vicki was distracted by listening to make sure the kids were okay. After a long week of work, and a difficult phone conversation with her mother, she wanted nothing more than to relax with a book. George, besides suffering from unfulfilled desires, had stubbed his toe on the table leg, and the pain made his request—"Sweetheart, can we talk?"—sound like a whine.

She tried giving him a dirty look, as if to say "Don't do this now." He launched into an explanation of all the work he'd been doing and how his need for passion was an intrinsic part of his love for her. She stiffened and stood up, but he kept going. She grabbed her keys and left.

George was stunned, then frantic. What if she never came back? Was this the end of their marriage? Where had she gone? Who was she seeing? He tried to stay calm as he served the children ice cream, telling them Vicki had gone to the store for something. In his mind, he was sure she'd gone to meet a lover or to flirt with strange men in a downtown bar.

In fact, he was closer to the truth when he lied to the kids. She went where she usually went when she had something on her mind—to the mall. Still fuming, she intended to go to the bookstore, to drink a cup of tea in the café and calm down.

On the way in, she spotted a clerk at a trendy shop, sporting bright blue hair. On any other day, it might have looked silly to her, but today it looked rebellious and sleek, with an air of "don't mess with me." In this mood, Vicki saw the blue hair as just the sort of statement she wanted to make, silent but bold. She strode decisively toward the beauty salon.

By the time Vicki was finally in the stylist's chair, she was beginning to calm down; she couldn't quite follow through on the decision to go blue. "Make it short," she said. In the context of her relationship, it was still a pointed statement. George had always found long hair sexy.

The new cut looked and felt great to Vicki. She tipped the stylist lavishly and headed back toward the bookstore. During the haircut, she'd remained silent, thinking. Maybe it *was* time to start figuring out what was wrong between her and George. He wasn't a bad guy; he was just driving her nuts.

At the bookstore, instead of heading for the café, Vicki strolled into the self-help section and began checking out books about marriage, sexuality, and relationships. One of them mentioned a word—"hypersexuality," meaning an unusually strong desire or pressure for sexual gratification—which reminded her of George. Vicki started looking the word up in various books, and she found that the symptom was associated with medical problems ranging from agitated depression to Parkinson's disease.

George may or may not have been truly hypersexual, but Vicki's reading helped her consider other explanations for his behavior. The possibility of a medical problem helped her to see him more sympathetically. She returned home, armed with a new book about relationships and resolved to bring a positive attitude to their discussion.

"Where in hell were *you?*" George hissed, controlling his volume because the children were in bed, but obviously enraged. "And what in hell is wrong with your hair?"

Vicki sighed—she really did like the haircut—and began reestablishing civil relations. "I'm sorry I walked out," she said, and she explained in a few simple words where she'd been. "I understand that you're angry, and I know this issue is important to you. Tonight wasn't the best time, but I do want to talk about this. Let's agree on a time and place where we can have the conversation we need to have."

They set up a meeting to talk about how to make their relationship better. Vicki said she wanted to hold this talk outside the home, because a neutral location would help them both focus. They agreed to go to a coffee shop the following weekend while the children were at a friend's house. George and Vicki decided on a time limit—forty-five minutes—and they acknowledged that this meeting wouldn't produce any instant cures, just start the process of healing.

To give them some structure for the meeting, Vicki suggested that they both go through the Consensus Questions, which she found in her book (also, see appendix), and to come to the meeting ready to talk about their answers. George made a tape recording of the questions so that it would be easier to answer in spoken words.

Vicki took some time alone with the tape after the kids were in bed, and the answers she gave reflected a lot of the thinking she did during her visit to the mall.

What do I really want? What is most important? "I really want some time to myself, without George pestering me, and the kids nagging me, and the house a mess, and the shop calling every twenty seconds. I want to be my own person. I am tired of being responsible for everything and everyone. But I also want George to love me just for who I *am*, not for what I *do*. I want to be considerate and fair, but I want to feel like I'm having a turn, too. I somehow feel like I've missed something important. I want to figure out what that is. What is most important, I think, is not torpedoing my marriage or hurting Sophy and Tim, but still finding a way to be more respectful of my own needs."

What right or rights do I want to exercise? What responsibilities go with them? "I want the right to make choices for me with my own timetable, needs, and goals. I want to make choices that help my children grow up strong and happy. I want not to have to worry as much as I do about other people's needs, especially people who are already adults.

"I guess I have the responsibility to choose wisely, after I consider things. I have the responsibility to remember that I have already made decisions that affect other people, like my children. I should try to make a reasonable effort to figure out what choices I want to make and not to expect anyone else to do it for me. I need to let others know what is going on with me and what I want them to do about it. If I choose something that affects other people, I do need to let them know about it!"

What kinds of pressure am I feeling? From whom? What does my partner seem to want? "I'm feeling pressured to be a 'good mom' and a 'good wife' and a 'good employer' and a 'good housekeeper.' Some of the pressure is from the people around me, and some of it is from inside me. I guess I feel that for some reason I have to prove I'm 'good,' but I'm also feeling pressure to say 'no' to anything anyone wants from me. George wants to get laid and to have things go back to the way they used to be. I think he really does want to understand me, but I hardly understand myself! And that feels like more pressure!"

What is my bottom line? Is this worth my while? "I guess my bottom line is—something has to change. Yes, it's worth my while, because I'll go crazy if things don't change."

What kind of time is involved here? Energy? Resources? "I really don't know what kind of time. I don't want a deadline that says that I have to be 'fixed' by a certain date. I guess I just don't have the energy to do what it feels like I need to do. I have so much else on my plate that I don't have time for me. Resources? Well, I do know that when I feel pressured I relieve my stress by shopping, and that isn't helping because I'm creating more bills."

What hasn't worked so far? What have I tried? What were the results? "Shopping. Cutting my hair. Working harder. Trying to pretend that everything is okay. Trying to get some time and space. Trying to communicate. Trying to make George do it my way. It seems like I just get to trusting that George is seeing me for who I am, like these past couple of weeks, and there he goes again about getting laid."

Have other people been in a similar situation? What did they try? Did it work? "Probably a million women have been where I am right now. I look at the divorce rate and figure that what they tried didn't work very well. My friend had this same kind of thing happen to her a couple of years ago, and she went to a therapy group. She hung in there and she and her boyfriend are still patching things up, but it has been really hard for them."

What approximates what I want? What conditions are present? "The past couple of weeks, George really has been trying to be more understanding and to be a better husband and father. I haven't been giving him a lot of encouragement because when I've praised his behavior in the past, he jumps to the assumption that I want to have sex."

What are some options? List at least three that are not mentioned above, including playful ones. "Well, I could give George sex without being interested, just 'lie back and think of England.' I could take a sabbatical from sex and be celibate for a time. I could hire a prostitute for him. Or I could get to the bottom of this and see what I can change in me."

George took the cassette on his drive to work. At first he was reluctant to put it into the player, to think and talk about his feelings instead of just relaxing to music as he usually did in the car. After a day or two, though, he listened to the questions, and he tried to answer them honestly. Once he began the exercise, he discovered that his answers came easily, in part because of the work he had already done.

What do I really want? What is most important? "I want to keep my marriage and my family. I want to be close, physically and emotionally, with my wife. I want to figure out what I did wrong. The most important thing is for us to work together to get through this."

What right or rights do I want to exercise? What responsibilities go with them? "I guess you might call them conjugal rights. We're married. We're supposed to be in love. We have great kids and a good life. I want to get some of my needs met, too, but I need to accept the responsibility for finding ways to make them not harmful to Vicki. The needs I feel sometimes overwhelm me, they are so intense. I don't want to lose that passion, but I do need to find a way to make it work for me, not against me or us."

What kinds of pressure am I feeling? From whom? What does my partner seem to want? "I'm feeling a man's pressure, responding to my wife whom I love. That's from inside me. I'm feeling pressure to be 'politically correct' and give her lots of room, even when I want to be close. Some of that pressure is from inside me, and some is from outside. I'm feeling pressure not to be a fool, like I was with my old girlfriend. I'm still worried that Vicki's seeing someone else. She doesn't seem to know what she wants, but it doesn't seem to be me!"

What is my bottom line? Is this worth my while? "Things have got to change. I want my family, but I want to be happy too. Yes, it really is worth my while."

What kind of time is involved here? Energy? Resources? "I don't know what kind of time we're talking about, but it seems like it should be soon. I'm using a lot of energy trying to be understanding and I'm tired. Resources? Not much, I think."

What hasn't worked so far? What have I tried? What were the results? "So far the things I've done seem to be absolutely ignored and unappreciated. I don't know what else to do."

Have other people been in a similar situation? What did they try? Did it work? "I guess they probably have. I don't know what they did, but being patient isn't getting me anywhere."

What approximates what I want? What conditions are pres-

ent? "When we were just going together, and before the kids came, we had the world's greatest relationship. We liked each other, we played, and we had sex. Even after Tim and Sophy came along, we still did things together. But over the past couple of years, it's been going downhill, even though there were some good times.

"When Vicki cut her hair, I was upset, and started in on her. But she said she was sorry for walking out, and I think she was really trying a little to understand me. I don't really know what to do."

What are some options? List at least three that are not mentioned above, including playful ones. "Well, there's always taking care of my own needs privately. Or I could join a monastery. Or I could take a mistress. But I don't like any of these."

The following weekend, George and Vicki met as they'd planned and talked about their answers. This was not easy. Vicki cried a couple of times, and she drew back once when George reached for her hand—but she stayed at the table.

They realized there was some common ground. They wanted to stay in the marriage, and neither of them wanted to go on with their current standoff. They wanted to be understood better. Neither wanted to hurt the other. Neither of them wanted a partner outside the marriage.

They agreed to meet again the following week to talk further. As a step toward trying not to be everything to everyone, Vicki decided she didn't want to be responsible for arranging child care for that meeting, so she asked George to do it. He was still hoping for more immediate changes, but he recognized that Vicki was going through a turbulent time and that she was trying to make things better. He felt powerless to help. Vicki spent the week thinking hard, trying to make sense of the jumble of feelings in her mind.

At their second meeting at the coffee shop, George and Vicki started a consensus negotiation. This was another tool explained in the book Vicki bought. They started by reestablishing the common ground from the last exercise and summed it up this way: "We both want to get our needs met while staying in this family and this marriage."

Next, they looked at what had changed or was about to change. In this case, the change had already occurred. They both had changed their priorities. They recognized this was natural and normal and that their job now was to find ways to acknowledge those priorities and to help each other.

What had changed? They talked about it until they came up with two statements they could agree on:

1. Vicki has become aware that she has changed since becoming a mother. She also notices that the time and energy she spends on taking care of the children has to come from somewhere. She also needs more personal time and space. The only place she sees some flexibility is around her sexuality and her role as a wife.

2. George, believing that their relationship was already firmly established, has in the past focused his energy on succeeding at work. When he reached that goal, he realized that the emptiness in his life was still not filled. Sexual problems are pointing him to the fact that he has been missing interactions with Vicki as his life partner.

Finally, they stated their individual priorities. Vicki wanted time for herself and freedom from pressure to perform. George wanted physical touch, to feel needed, to make progress in solving the problem. They each wanted to be better understood by the other.

Vicki and George came away from the meeting feeling they had made a step forward; they had been able to communicate their own needs and emotions without being blamed or judged. George even noticed that Vicki seemed a little more relaxed in his presence. This time he knew better than to reach for her, and while it was frustrating not to be able to hold her, it also felt good to see her lose some of her tension and nervousness.

The next step was to set up another meeting to try to craft a solution. George had seen progress in himself after doing some spiritual work, and he suggested the same tools, Tarot and spellwork, might work for the two of them together. Vicki agreed and said she would take her turn at setting up a sitter. She asked that they continue not to meet at home. Instead, they decided to go to a picnic area on the outskirts of town.

They brought some sandwiches, a bottle of wine, and a small Tarot deck. Before their meal, they sat down at a secluded table to do the One-Card Meditation (see appendix). George drew the Moon card. On his first journey into the card, he focused on the moon herself—light but not necessarily warm, a solemn face. In their Wiccan practice George had become familiar with many aspects of moon symbolism, and this card reminded him of all of them—femininity, change, mystery. To him, this moon represented Vicki.

THE MOON.

Next, he focused on the dogs howling at the moon. They could make all the noise they liked, but they wouldn't change anything about the moon. To him, they represented himself.

Finally, he became aware of the landscape—a path leading from a body of water through a field to mountains beyond. His three options came out of this last experience:

1. Follow the long road to the mountain, the most difficult path, which represents the hard work of rebuilding their marriage.
2. Dive into the water; swim away from the cold moon, leaving the marriage in body or spirit.
3. Remain in the grassy area, an easy choice of simply accepting things the way they are.

Vicki drew the 4 of Pentacles. She was first drawn to the glum central figure in the card, clinging tightly to his riches despite no apparent threat. To her, this resonated with her own clinging to her sexuality as an area of life she could control, despite the fact that no one in her life now, least of all George, intended to harm her.

Next, she saw the city behind the central figure, which to her represented new adventures. She realized that her trip to the hairdresser a few weeks earlier was the first time she'd felt adventurous in a long time.

Her final meditation produced nothing much of value to her, but Vicki was aware of being part of a pattern, that many people before had felt like she was feeling, had drawn this card and found truth in it.

She came up with the following options:

1. Consolidate her "treasures"—her time, energy, and body. Refuse to let go of any more than she has to.
2. Leave behind old patterns, changing her behavior the way she changed her hair.
3. Find a new balance between keeping and giving.

The cards, and the structure of the exercise, helped George and Vicki focus their energies and emotions. At the end, when they were left simply looking at each other across a battered picnic table, Vicki began to cry. George again wanted to put his arms around her, to fix whatever was wrong for her. Yet he didn't know whether it was something he *could* fix, and he knew from their conversations that she experienced his physical affection as more pressure. So he stayed on his side of the table and asked, "Do you want me to hold you?" Given the freedom to make a choice, she thought about it and nodded her head "yes." She pulled away after a few seconds, but that brief contact gave George some much-needed encouragement.

When Vicki had calmed down, they opened their basket and began to eat and talk. George and Vicki decided that they wouldn't try to change everything at once. Instead, they planned to make a list of a few small changes, to try them for a month, and to meet again and find out what did and didn't work.

To give Vicki some free time, George offered to take sole responsibility for the children one night a week, so that she could go out and do whatever she wanted to do for herself, with no household responsibilities. He asked her to choose which night so that he could let his office know he would not be available for late projects on that day. This sounded wonderful to Vicki. She chose Mondays, which were usually slow at her shop. Because she wanted to reassure him that she wasn't seeing another man, she offered to let him know where she would be.

Then George asked Vicki to find some way to support him in meeting his need for physical affection and sexual release. Vicki grew tense and silent. George remained calm but did not back down from the request. He asked her to look again at the options they came up with. What would work best, given that his needs were not going to go away?

"All right," she said finally. "I guess it's not reasonable to expect you to wait for me. If you need time alone to take care of your needs, let me know." She promised to keep the children out of his way for an hour or so. George said he would need to purchase some magazines or movies for his private pleasures, but he promised to keep them discreetly out of sight. He asked her to think about doing something more to be present in this part of his life—perhaps taking a role in setting the scene for his "alone time." She made no promises.

That still left him with a strong need to be touched. He asked her to think about a way she could touch him and feel comfortable doing so. He now knew that she experienced his touch as pressure or "pestering," so he agreed that any touching she did would not be interpreted as sexual, that he would not try to take it any further.

"I guess I could give you a back rub," she said. "You liked it when we took that massage class together a few years ago." Yes, he had, but that was because the class usually left them both feeling turned on. He kept this thought to himself and agreed that a back rub would be welcome. They made a deal that she would give him a back rub twice a week for twenty minutes.

It wasn't perfect. Neither of them had gotten everything they wanted. George would have preferred to enjoy sexual relations with Vicki. Vicki would have preferred not to do any touching at all. At the same time, they were each getting something they did need. In Vicki's case, it was Monday nights "off." In George's case, it was two back rubs a week, plus acknowledgment that he needed time for his sexual outlet. They shook hands and set up another meeting for four weeks later.

Vicki told George, "I know it's important that I talk with you about my feelings, but it's also really hard for me." She suggested they use the tools of ritual to empower this part of their lives, and together they devised a Spell of Communication (see appendix). Vicki said the spell helped her feel clearer, and that simply devoting time and energy to the goal of better communication was a way to help bring about that reality. George didn't feel much different when it was done, but he appreciated her willingness to work on her own obstacles.

The Power of Consensus

When partners learn to make decisions together, each choice they make builds on a foundation of honor and respect, sustaining and improving the relationship between them. They start with respecting each partner's right to equal time, energy, and resources. They give each other the gift of recognizing their own preferences and goals—the preferences and goals of their partners and the ones they have in common. They choose to build a shared path in which each person's needs are honored.

The negotiation process outlined here is most useful when both partners recognize that their goal is not to "win," but to reach an agreement that best satisfies everyone. As the story of Marie and Richard illustrated, many times simple tools can help clarify choices and eliminate outside influences.

Consensus is ultimately about giving your relationship priority. This is not sacrificing yourself for your partner, but giving your energy to that which sustains and energizes you both. When consensus is working well, everyone benefits.

Consensus decisions are often most difficult to bring up, and most valuable to make, when the issues are the most serious. Here, Cynthia describes how such a decision became, literally, a lifesaver.

—————————— *Cynthia Speaks* ——————————

When my husband Chris was near the end of his illness, I wrote this:

March 18, 1998

Earlier today I met two fellow coven members at a restaurant to talk about Chris.

Chris and I have discussed at some length the possibility of using a medication overdose (methadone or morphine or both) if the time should come that he were in pain that he was not able to handle.

We also agreed there would be a waiting period of at least twenty-four hours from the time that Chris requested the overdose until it would be administered. This would allow loved ones to gather and to be with him at his passing, and also would allow time to be sure this choice came from unrelenting pain rather than depression or self-pity. Finally, we planned to use this time for me to say my good-byes to Chris privately and for him to make final preparations.

My covenmates have again raised the question of giving him an overdose. My agreement with Chris does not include administering an overdose myself. It merely allowed me to help him if he decided to take one. My covenmates, who also care about Chris, are encouraging me to consider going further. The complexity of the question is overwhelming for me. I am very clear about several things and very foggy on everything else.

I know that my first choice is for the Goddess to take Chris when I am present by simply allowing him to go to sleep and stop breathing.

I know that if I choose to supply an overdose to Chris, I guarantee a peaceful and easy death for him.

I know that by not choosing to overdose Chris, I am choosing to risk a lingering or horrible death for him.

I know that if Chris were in pain that the medication could not control, I would not hesitate to overdose him after a twenty-four-hour wait.

I know that whatever I choose, I will accept both the responsibility and the consequences.

I know that Chris said to me today that he was not in physical pain and that he did not want me to overdose him, because he was not ready to pass. I believe he was fully aware of what he was saying and that his answers were not forced.

I know I have issues of my own that may be clouding my judgment, my ability to discern, and my choices. I believe that I am making honest efforts to work these out. However, I also believe that my own blindness to my issues may leave me in karmic debt, as I have not done what I needed to do to make the best decisions regarding Chris's life and death.

I am afraid that if I do overdose Chris, I will be forcing the Goddess's hand, condemning him to another turn on the wheel because he has unfinished business, that I will go to jail for murder, or that I will have arrogantly chosen a path for another.

I am afraid that if I don't overdose Chris, I will be the instrument of a death that condemns him or me to another turn on the wheel, that I will be guilty of a lack of love and compassion, or that again I will have arrogantly chosen a path for another.

I vowed to Chris that I would be present for him in five ways.

I consider Chris my equal in value. His comfort, his freedom, his choices are as important as mine. My comfort, my freedom, my choices are as important as his.

I choose our path by consensus. I am not clearly convinced that it is time to provide an overdose, and what I hear from him is that he does not want me to.

I have vowed to be emotionally honest. I can be nowhere but where I am. I am afraid, confused, hurt, miserable, pressured, tired, sorry, guilty, and exhausted.

I give and receive freely. I cannot freely give the overdose.

I esteem him as my primary relationship. I must choose for him and for me first, not for my family or his, or for our friends or the medical people.

And tonight, in the absence of a clear heart and in presence of great fear and confusion, I choose to err—if error it be—on the side of caution and inaction. The twenty-four hours has not yet begun.

It never did begin. Chris died two days later, naturally and peacefully, in his sleep.

Telling Your Truth

The Principle of Honesty

All of us have emotions, and our emotional lives are an important part of who we are. In a healthy relationship, partners are free to talk honestly about what they feel, believe, and think. They take responsibility for their own reactions and emotions, and they work to stay in touch with their own feelings and those of their partner. In such a relationship, partners need not hide nor gloss over their anger, fear, sadness, or other "negative" emotions. They can speak truthfully while acknowledging and caring about each other in a genuine way.

Chapter 1 talked about being honest with yourself, working to understand your own truth. Chapter 2 discussed using that truth to make decisions together. With these two pieces in place, in an atmosphere of trust and respect, it becomes possible for that truth to take a central place in your relationship.

To honor the West, the place of feelings and relationships, we are **emotionally honest with ourselves and each other.** We commit to being open to change, to the process of facing and accepting uncomfortable emotions in ourselves and each other. We tell each other the truth about ourselves, even when it is difficult.

Emotional Honesty

More than any other part of this book, the work of emotional honesty is founded in love. It takes a leap of faith to drop your defenses and trust your partner with the feelings, thoughts, dreams, ideas, and words that are most essentially yours.

Emotional honesty isn't achieved simply or quickly. It takes work, work that will go on for the rest of your relationship, both with yourself and with your partner. This work has two parts: affirming your own growing and spiritual self, and at the same time staying connected to others, no matter where they are in their lives.

It is no trouble at all to stay "connected" to family, friends, or partners when we are walking the same paths and remembering similar experiences. It is more difficult to remain connected while we try to define our experiences and ourselves in new ways, to embark on new phases of life, or to change old patterns.

All of us build defenses to protect parts of ourselves. We trade away parts of ourselves to survive in a world that often seems hostile and dangerous. Because we need to bring our whole selves to the work of emotional honesty, we'll devote a significant part of this section to recognizing what prevents us from knowing our own hearts.

Being emotionally honest with your partner does not mean you have to lay bare your entire self. No matter how deep your relationships, your emotions remain your own. Many things about you are unknown to your partner, and many things about your partner remain unknown to you, no matter how long you have been together. In a healthy relationship, small mysteries and surprises are a source of delight and intrigue. You have every right to keep some parts of yourself private.

In keeping with the information on codependency in this section, though, make sure your decisions honor yourself and your truth, not what your partner might think and do. In keeping with your own ethical system, consider the consequences of what you withhold. Sharing information about your feelings is difficult—but so is dealing with the misunderstandings that build up when you don't share.

Emotional honesty means a commitment to communicate your feelings and thoughts to your partner in matters that concern you both. You take a risk by speaking your truth without trying to anticipate your partner's response. It takes energy and effort to learn to speak your truth without harmful words. It takes strength and trust to accept the gift of truth from your partner, even when it sometimes makes you feel angry or sad or afraid. Over time this becomes easier, and partners with the habit of emotional honesty gain from understanding each other rather than protecting each other from the truth.

The truth can often be painful. Sharing that pain honestly can help partners feel protected and loved even when it can't take the pain away.

Emotional Dishonesty

We may learn to ignore our perceptions, our creativity, or our needs because others disregard us, ridicule us, or impose their standards on us. We may learn to be physically ill because it gives emotional comfort. We may try to please others in the hope that perhaps, maybe, finally, it will be our turn.

Sometimes being intimate with ourselves and honoring that can be pretty simple. Look at the following example:

Brett and five friends have just had a great lunch together. Someone suggests a movie, and the others chime in with their approval. But something inside Brett starts twitching and he realizes he simply doesn't want to go.

If he were practicing emotional honesty as soon as he noticed his emotions, he'd probably say something like this before the decision was made: "I really like being with you all, and I don't want our time to end. But for some reason—and I have no idea what it is—I just don't want to go to the movies. Is anyone up for something else?"

It is a lot more likely that his dialogue would be mostly internal. His thoughts might include: *I don't want to break up the fun I've been enjoying with these great people. All of them want to go, so who am I to rain on their parade? I can't make up my mind. Should I go along with the group? I really don't have any plans or pressing needs, the movie sounds okay, and I really want some more time with them. What if I say no? I don't want them to think I don't like being with them.*

If he goes, he may well end up resenting the trip and his friends. Or he may have a great time. The point is that he has harmed himself by not speaking up. Every time he fails to acknowledge and honor his truth, he gives away a part of himself. If he does that often enough, he gets spiritually, emotionally, and physically drained and sick.

Myth: The Locked Room

The Slavic story of Marya Morevna is a twist on a standard folktale theme. Prince Ivan went to seek his fortune, came across a battlefield after the fight was over, and discovered that the winning general was a princess, Marya Morevna. The princess, a woman of action, saw Ivan, liked what she saw, and immediately invited him to her tent. Shortly thereafter, they were married, and they settled down in her realm.

After a period of domestic bliss, Marya Morevna wanted to

return to the battlefield. She asked Ivan to care for her household in her absence, gave him the keys to everything, and placed only one restriction on him: There was one room he was not to enter under any circumstances.

Ivan was only human. He couldn't resist looking in that room. In fact, he barely waited till she was out of sight. Inside, a prisoner hung on the wall, bound by twelve chains. The man begged Ivan piteously to bring him some water. "Why not?" said Ivan, and he brought him a bucketful. The prisoner drank it and begged for more. After the third bucket, he regained his strength, burst the chains, and proclaimed, "Thanks, Ivan! Now you will sooner see your own ears than Marya Morevna!" For the prisoner was her worst enemy, Koschei the Deathless, who sped away to capture Marya Morevna and imprison her in his turn.

Ivan found her eventually. (And the first thing she said was, "Why did you disobey me?") After many adventures, the enemy was slain and they lived happily-ever-after.

Still, wouldn't it have been easier if Marya Morevna had told her husband what was in the room in the first place? Most of us don't have vanquished foes chained in the basement. (If you do, don't tell us, okay?) We do, however, keep parts of ourselves locked away from our partners. It's natural and normal to do so. We have reasons for the emotional boundaries we set, as well as experiences that extend before and beyond our partners' knowledge of us.

Quite often, though, it becomes clear that we're hanging on to information our partners need to know. Telling your truth can prevent many a long, perilous journey. Part of emotional dishonesty is failing to give information your partner needs to fully understand and love you.

USING YOUR WORDS

Sometimes it is easier to begin the emotionally honest dialogue with a preface. It might be a simple statement, such as "If I could wave my magic wand we would go for a walk instead of to the movies," or "I'm feeling cranky today, and I'd rather not sit in a movie theater."

However, it is also possible to do too much prefacing, as this next story illustrates.

Dora and Nicole had been living together for several months. Nicole had arrived home early, cooked dinner, and eagerly awaited Dora's arrival. Dora came in a bit later than usual, and almost as soon as she walked in the door Nicole felt a distance in their greeting. By the time dinner was over, Nicole was distraught. Dora said, "Honey, we need to talk."

Nicole's heart plummeted to her shoes, fearing that her partner was going to dump her. Dora went on at some length about work, finances, and her friend's new baby. All the while, poor Nicole sat in fear, trying to guess what was really going on. Eventually (and it seemed like hours later to Nicole) Dora delivered her bombshell: She really didn't want to hurt her lover's feelings, but she thought the soup Nicole had fixed for dinner was too spicy.

Nicole was relieved, but also irritated and bewildered. For one thing, Dora had said she liked the soup last time. Wouldn't it have been simpler for Dora to say at the first presentation of the soup, without criticism, "If I could change just one thing, it would be to make this great soup less spicy so that I could enjoy the vegetables"? As we have mentioned in the preceding chapters, to deny that there is a problem is to set yourself and your partner up for serious misunderstandings.

This is a relatively trivial example, but it points to some important aspects of emotional honesty. There were two factors that meant that emotional honesty could not or would not occur until something significant changed.

First, Dora assumed that she could hurt Nicole's feelings. Often, if we know someone well, we can predict how that person will react. From this, it's far too easy a step to feel that we "made" him or her feel that way. If we insist on taking responsibility for someone else's feelings, we have to censor our own truth.

Second, Dora had not told the truth the first time. This is the pattern we described earlier: giving away parts of oneself in order to—we believe—survive. On that day, her need to be close to Nicole had seemed greater than her need to have soup she could enjoy. Nicole failed to tell the truth when she didn't talk about her uncomfortable feeling of distance. The longer we let something go without tending to it, the bigger and messier it becomes.

HURT AND HARM

We do *not* have the power to hurt anyone's feelings. We can certainly set up the circumstances that may result in hurt feelings, but we truly can't hurt someone else's feelings. We can prove that to you, right here, in print. Remember, we're warning you that this is a setup!

Imagine that you and I are in the same room, and you are wearing a sweater. I look at the sweater and you and say "I like your sweater." How do you respond?

Now, remembering that we just told you that you were being set up, you might be suspicious and consider your answer for a moment or two. What can possibly happen? Most people answer with some form of "thank you," as it seems a relatively safe answer.

And so it is. But you could have felt or said any of these things:

"This old thing? I just threw it on!"

"Every time someone says something nice about something I have, they want to borrow it!"

"Oh, no! She knows I stole it!"

"Oh, I'm so glad! I really needed to hear that I chose the right thing to wear. I agonized for hours."

"She is pretty quick on the uptake, realizing that this sweater matches the ceremonial magic day correspondence."

Your experiences, perceptions, and desires all influence what you feel. The comment on your sweater is merely the opportunity for you to respond. The person making the comment doesn't *make* you feel one way or another, pleased or guilty or defensive or whatever. You made yourself feel that way. Likewise, I can't make you angry, sad, or happy. Only you can choose those feelings in response to the world around you.

We often assume others feel and respond as we do. If I enjoy being pampered when I am sick, I may offer the same treatment to you. If you like being alone in your misery, I may feel terribly neglected when you give me the same space for my illness. If you enjoy being complimented on your wit, you may give such compliments to me, unless I let you know that I experience the praise as pressure to perform.

On the opposite end of the scale, it's possible to use your truth deliberately to injure someone. This is verbal abuse, and it, too, eliminates the possibility of honesty.

Here's a way to figure out the difference: If you tell me the soup I made is too spicy, I may feel hurt, but the hurt feelings are my chosen response based on the associations your words evoke in me. My feelings can get hurt if I make assumptions or read meaning into your words. By focusing on a behavior, object, or situation, you may allow me an interpretation that leaves my feelings unhurt.

Harming someone with words, speaking in a way that clearly indicates scorn for the recipient as a person—for instance, "You're too stupid to cook right"—can be as destructive as physically hitting that person. Such behavior offers no chance to build truth or trust.

Codependency and Health

The problem of "giving away parts of oneself" was defined a few years ago as "codependency." You may have heard this word before. It's been used about many different behaviors, families, and attitudes. Though the term has been seriously overused, there is still some value in it.

Unfortunately, many books and experts define codependency so broadly that saying "thank you" might easily qualify one as a codependent! Another problem is that many of the behaviors defined as codependent are simply good manners, or appropriate for one who is responsible for other people (such as a parent, guardian, or health care professional).

The word *codependency* grew out of behavioral scientists' observations of families in which one or more members had a substance abuse problem. They noticed that spouses, children, or other relatives would protect an addict from the consequences of his or her addiction. More important, such protectors often would derive their personal sense of worth from these actions.

Very soon it became clear that this behavior was widespread even when no chemical dependency was present. Codependency refers to dependence on others' reinforcement rather than acting from inner self-worth—being other-centered rather than self-centering.

Before we describe codependency further, a word of warning: You may recognize yourself here even if you're emotionally healthy. Many behaviors defined as codependent are only harmful when carried to extremes or when they create a barrier blocking real feelings and perceptions. If we use these behaviors 20 percent of the time, there is probably nothing to be concerned about. If they are true for us more than half the time, then perhaps we need to look at them more carefully.

Codependency is rooted in shame, not guilt. Guilt happens when you do something wrong. If you are guilty, you can correct the problem by making amends. Shame occurs when you feel that you *are* something wrong. If you feel shame, no matter what the source, you cannot correct it or move on. You are stuck.

Codependency harms both oneself and others. If Lucy "protects" her children from knowing that money is tight by spending too much on holiday gifts, she is setting them up to expect the world to do the same thing. And she is setting them up to whine when other material wants run up against the reality of a depleted checkbook.

I might try to "protect" you by not telling you the truth about a friend's illness. That harms me, because I have to spend energy guarding the secret when I could be finding comfort in discussing my worries. It also harms you, by depriving you of the opportunity to react to the truth, and harms our friend by depriving her of your sympathy and understanding.

Or I might insist you do something my way when you are really able to or should choose for yourself. Dean buys Bonnie all-natural toothpaste at the store, even though he knows she's been using another brand. The brand he bought feels harsh to Bonnie's teeth, and she wishes he'd respected her choice.

The motivations behind these things are not bad, but the results are. An extreme case was written up several years ago: A child attended a birthday party and enjoyed too much ice cream, cake, and candy. As kids often will, the child became cranky because of the "sugar high." An adult, exhibiting codependency by assuming her body was the proper standard, wanted to "help" the child by adding protein to her system. The adult offered the child some crackers with peanut butter. The child refused, saying she wasn't allowed to have them. The adult insisted that the child eat the crackers. The child was highly allergic to peanuts and went into respiratory arrest. Both the child and the adult were harmed!

Modern Western culture reinforces many codependent behaviors. Such behaviors begin when we are afraid of something—rejection, pain, falling, being hungry, not knowing the answer. Our fears awaken the most basic part of our brains, and we find ourselves doing one of the preprogrammed "f" responses—"fight," "flight," or (to put it politely) "fornicate." Because we are not as a rule menaced by saber-toothed tigers, we respond by giving away some portion of ourselves in order to deal with the problem.

For instance, we "fight" by becoming insistent that we will eat all we want, even if we have to sneak into the kitchen at night. Here we begin the ethical compromises: disobedience, lying, stealing, and harming ourselves by ignoring our bodies and reacting to the threat we perceive. Or we insist we will get perfect grades in school, and we will condemn ourselves if we don't. To obtain the good grades, we may ignore health and balance in our lives, cheat on tests, pretend to be interested in a subject, or look down on others who don't do as well.

We choose "flight" by becoming more accommodating, or nicer, and push down or deny our own feelings in the process. We learn quickly that by giving our genuine opinion about the food on the table, we may receive a reprimand, no dessert, or ridicule. We learn to hide our desire to date an attractive person because he or she doesn't seem interested. In many situations, society tells us that being attracted to persons of one's own gender is wrong, so we become wary of even forming close friendships.

Or we "fornicate," seeking distance from our fear in some kind of endorphin rush like that of a sexual climax, though it may take the form of shopping, driving too fast, bulimia, drug abuse, or other harmful behaviors. As we separate ourselves from our fear, we also move away from our inner selves, our spirituality. The further we are from our spiritual center, the more likely we are to suffer a loss of personal morality. At the very least, we are lying to others and ourselves. Intimacy cannot come from lies.

CATEGORIES OF CODEPENDENCY

Codependent behaviors are so many and so widespread that it's possible to group them into categories that correspond to the cardinal points of a sacred circle. Each one corresponds to a Principle.

East: Boundaries

This is about knowing where oneself ends and other people start. Larry tells his kids to put on sweaters when *he* is cold. He pretends to believe some things because he doesn't want to hurt people's feelings. He has compromised things he shouldn't have in order to keep the peace or avoid hurting someone. Even if he knows someone isn't telling the truth, he'd rather let it go than confront it. It's easy for Larry to take responsibility for the actions of others so that they won't have it so hard—he knows they didn't mean to do the wrong thing.

If you identify with a lot of issues in these areas, the Principle of Equals might be a fruitful idea to explore in your relationships.

South: Control and Perfectionism

Vanessa worries about a lot of different things over which she has no influence. She feels she must always be in control, as if the world would stop if she stopped doing what people expect of her. She insists some things must be done a certain way, and ends up doing them herself. Vanessa needs to keep parts of her life just as they are so that she doesn't get too off-balance.

For her, people and situations tend to be right or wrong, black or white. She has a hard time setting realistic goals for herself. She feels much guiltier than most people would if she makes a mistake. Her family couldn't get along without her. She works and worries so long and hard that she is exhausted, but she still finds a way to do a little bit more.

Someone with strong issues in this area might benefit from examining the Consensus issues in relationships.

West: Neglecting, Exaggerating, or Minimizing Oneself

Brian's feelings are either very intense or not there at all, and often he doesn't know what he feels. He finds himself thinking about hurtful things from the past. He has a hard time trying to sort out what is really going on. He tends to ignore his intuition to make decisions based on what seems rational, even if it means he is harmed in the process. He is afraid to pay too much attention to his feelings when making a decision.

He feels he would be nothing without his most important relationships. He believes his partner needs him more than he needs his partner. He would rather take care of someone else than be taken care of himself. He lets his needs and wants go by the wayside so he can take care of others' needs and wants first. The worst thing he can imagine is being alone. Yet he doesn't have someone to whom he can really tell everything.

Emotional Honesty is the Principle most closely related to this area of codependency.

North: Impression Management

It is very important that people believe Wendy is a good person. She keeps up a good front, though she doesn't feel she is worth much. It is easier for her to be kind and forgiving to others than to herself. She will spend much more effort than necessary so other people will think well of her. Wendy has a hard time accepting compliments because she doesn't think she deserves them. Even if she doesn't feel well, she finds herself saying, "I'm fine."

If Wendy is going out to eat with others, she will never be the one to choose the restaurant. She lets other choose, partly because she really doesn't know what she'd like, and partly because she wants the others to be pleased. She is uncomfortable with trusting what she sees or understands unless someone else sees or understands the same thing.

If this sounds familiar, you may wish to focus on issues around the Principle of Giving and Receiving.

Center: Fear of Not Being Enough or Having Enough

Peter's emotions prevent his having a healthy relationship with food. Money is a continual source of worry for him. He has a sense that there is something basically wrong with him. When things are really bad, Peter wonders why these things don't seem to happen to others, but always to him. He has trouble either sleeping too much or not enough. Things that he used to enjoy are not as much fun as they were before.

Peter is prone to physical pain and illness. His energy level is nearly zero, even though he tries very hard to meet his responsibilities. He is not as close to the Divine as he'd like to be. He has a hard time making changes. The family he grew up in never understood him. Peter feels used.

For people like Peter, the Principle of Balance is a possible starting point for working to make things better.

Jane Speaks

Okay, go back and skim over all those codependent behaviors, and you'll have an excellent idea what I was like in my first serious relationship. I was the codependency poster child. Essentially, I gave away a large part of myself in order to keep the relationship together. His emotions, problems, and projects took up a large part of my energy and time as well as his own. My own needs, wants, and fears seemed less important, and I stifled my growing unhappiness and anger for months that stretched into years.

With all that was not being said, the atmosphere between us became highly charged. Small things took on unnatural importance. He didn't want to go grocery shopping, and I took it as a sign that he hated me. He criticized me for snapping at a store clerk, and I thought he was ashamed to be with me. I responded by giving up even more to try to make him happy.

By the end of our time together, we were barely speaking to each other. We took on extra projects to get out of the house because we didn't want to be there together. Eventually, another man's attentions gave me some hint of the fun I was missing. All that anger found expression as I cheated on my partner and then broke off the relationship.

The new relationship was brief, and I found myself alone and unhappy. I determined never to behave that way again. I knew I had to find out where I had gone wrong. I talked with many people, did some reading, and realized some of my mistakes. I consciously set out to learn what makes a relationship work, and I discovered that taking better care of my own emotions was an important part of it.

I'm still working on it. I've made some changes in myself and have a wonderful partner to share my life. I probably still make ''codependent'' decisions every day. But I have learned more about telling my partner what I feel, and hearing what he feels.

Happily-Ever-After

The following couple is working to hear each other:

Anne and Philip, both in their early thirties, had just gotten engaged. It was a thrilling time for both. Philip was in the middle of a medical internship, and he planned his residency in a city far from their hometown. Anne, a music teacher, was looking forward to the wedding and their new life, though it would mean leaving the Wiccan coven that had been important to her for the past three years.

The trouble arose the first time they visited Philip's parents after announcing their engagement. "Have you set a date yet?" asked Donna, Philip's mother. "You'd better start reserving soon—I know St. Agatha's has to be booked months in advance, and of course you'll want Father Bernard. Shall I call him for you?"

Philip started to nod agreement, then caught sight of Anne's look of dismay. Hoping to avoid a confrontation, he said, "Oh, thank you, Mother, but Anne and I really need to do some planning together before we make any reservations."

Donna was vaguely dissatisfied, but she dropped the subject. Joe, Philip's father, said, "We want you two to have the best, and I hope you know your mother and I will be helping pay for everything." This was only reasonable. Philip came from a well-to-do family, and their help meant Anne could pursue a music career instead of seeking dull, higher paying employment to fund his schooling. While Joe and Donna had always been welcoming, Anne had often felt the difference between their life and the hand-to-mouth existence of her own upbringing.

On the way back from his parents' home, Anne told Philip she was not willing to be married in a Catholic ceremony. She liked his family and didn't want to offend them, but her own faith was too important to sacrifice.

Philip was torn. He had been brought up Catholic, had moved away from religion in his twenties, and now considered himself an agnostic. He supported Anne's religious path, attending occasional ceremonies with her and making himself well liked among her Wiccan friends.

Philip also understood his parents' point of view. Until now, he and Anne had agreed not to discuss Wicca with his family, not wishing to offend them. Joe and Donna, meanwhile, had assumed their future daughter-in-law was a Christian. They'd even seen a statue of St. Brigit in Philip and Anne's home. They had no reason to believe a Catholic wedding would be offensive.

Now, however, it seemed conflict was inevitable. Philip asked what sort of wedding Anne wanted, hoping he could figure out a compromise. Ideally, she said, they would be married by Ed and Jackie, her High Priest and Priestess, in a ceremony honoring the Goddess and God who were patrons of her coven. Philip knew and liked the coven leaders, but he also knew how horrified his family would be at this idea. Then Anne turned the tables: What kind of wedding did he want? He didn't care. He wanted everyone to be happy.

The next day, still troubled by their talk, Anne took out her Tarot cards and did the Four Points of Perspective exercise for her relationship with Philip.

As Anne sees herself. The reversed 4 of Pentacles indicates "suspense, delay, opposition." Anne was suspended in time while she and Philip struggled with this decision, in which her wishes and those of his parents were opposed.

As Anne sees Philip.   In the reversed position the 9 of Pentacles can indicate "bad faith." While she respected Philip's need to honor his parents, Anne also couldn't help feeling a little betrayed. She expected that as a soon-to-be-married couple, they would put each other first, and she wished he had been more interested in making a decision together rather than keeping the peace.

As Philip sees Anne.   Here Anne was startled to find that on some level, her fiancé saw her as a source of discord and financial stress. Looking at the dispute through his eyes, she saw herself as a troublemaker.

As Philip sees himself.   The mixed meanings of this card evoked some interesting thoughts for Anne: money (the unspoken hold Philip's parents had over the young couple), an altercation (the family quarrel Philip sought to avoid at all costs), and ingenuity (his hope that they could dream up a solution that would satisfy everyone).

In addition, the all-Pentacles nature of this reading told Anne that money was more important to this issue than either of them had admitted. She decided to specifically address that issue when they talked together.

Next, she did the exercise for her own relationship with Joe, Philip's father:

As Anne sees herself.   In this relationship she felt like a source of discord and a financial drain.

As Anne sees Joe.   He was stagnant, not open to new ideas or the possibility that his way wasn't the only way.

As Joe sees Anne.   The card indicates tears and sadness. Was Joe sad at the prospect of his son's marriage? Or was Joe afraid that Philip would be sad?

As Joe sees himself.   Joe saw himself as successful in business, and he drew a great deal of meaning out of being able to win negotiations. This was an "aha!" card for Anne. She realized that working out a solution involving Joe would have to include some point on which he could "win."

Finally, she examined her relationship with Donna, Philip's mother:

As Anne sees herself.   Again the 7 of Wands, but this time it was Anne herself who felt triumphant and successful. Anne realized that because of her creative work, she felt superior to Donna, whose primary career had been as a homemaker. Anne

didn't like what this told her about herself, and she made a note to examine her own behavior toward Donna to make sure she wasn't patronizing the older woman.

As Anne sees Donna.   The card indicated "trickery, artifice, fraud," which puzzled Anne. She had always perceived Donna as being genuine and honest. Then she realized that the card referred to Donna's emphasis on appearances, on doing what was expected. Donna would honestly rather see Philip married in a ceremony that meant nothing to him and Anne, if the alternative meant defying the expectations of her relatives and friends.

As Donna sees Anne.   The card of heartbreak! Here Anne saw Donna's real fears for her son. She had trouble trusting that any woman was good enough for her son, and she feared Philip would be unhappy in his marriage and his new life. Anne also saw an alternative meaning indicating Donna's own sadness at "losing" her son as he grew up.

As Donna sees herself.   In this card Anne saw Donna struggling in a codependent attempt to make everyone happy. Not for the first time Anne recognized the same quality in her future husband!

Anne came away from this exercise with some added insight into Philip and his parents. The reading helped her to see that Joe and Donna were not simply adhering to convention at all costs. They genuinely wanted to see their son happy, and they were sad at the prospect of losing him not only to a faraway city but to a new wife. The readings also helped Anne to see that she and Philip needed to have a conversation about the financial side of their wedding.

Armed with this information, Anne asked Philip to set aside some time to talk. They needed to make some decisions about their wedding, but they also knew those decisions must be ones each could honestly support in the face of pressure from outside their relationship. They decided to talk through their concerns using the Honesty Questions and the Ritual of Listening, found in the *Spellbook* (see appendix), which were standard procedures for resolving conflicts in Anne's coven.

They began by reflecting separately on the Honesty Questions. When they sat down together a few days later, Anne took the lead in putting the problem on the table. What follows are the statements they made. For each statement, they went through the restatement and correction process described in the *Spellbook* (see appendix), using sentences that began "I hear you saying ———."

Part 1 (Anne states the issue in her words).   "I'm not ashamed of who I am! I used to be concerned that other people would put me down for my religion, but not anymore. I've gone through doubts about this path, but I'm clear now: I'm a practicing Wiccan.

"When we started talking about the wedding with your folks, I knew we would not be in agreement. They are sincere in their faith, and I respect their right to choose it, but I don't feel any connection to Catholic beliefs or attitudes. I don't wish to be married in a ceremony that doesn't mean anything to me, that reflects spiritual ideas that are so different from my own.

"I really don't want your parents to be upset. I really like them and they are making it possible for you to go to medical school. I know that they're not trying to hurt me; they care about you and want you to be happy. And I really want us to get along with your family.

"I had something similar to this situation with my last serious boyfriend. I was willing to go along with his family to services on Christmas (which I just saw as polite, and not a religious thing). And from that he got the idea that he could pressure me into giving up the things that he didn't think were all that important, like time with my girlfriends. The weird thing is that it wasn't about religion with him: that was just an excuse to control me. I'm afraid that if I go along with a Catholic wedding, it will mean that I lose a part of myself.

"I really want to make things easy for you, because I love you. But this is a place that I can't and won't compromise. I am afraid that if anything goes wrong at the wedding, it will be my fault and I'll be in for some rough times. I am also afraid that by carrying a lot of the cost, your parents are somehow 'buying' the right to decide what kind of wedding we have.

"I want a ceremony that is meaningful for both of us, one that affirms our love and commitment. I want Ed and Jackie to perform it because they are the ones who have stood by me spiritually in good times and in not-so-good times. And they know and love you, too. I don't want some stranger who might think of women as second class to set the tone for our life together. And I want you to be committed to what we choose, and to choose us first, even if it means going against your parents' wishes."

Part 1 (Philip states the issue in his words).   "I guess I'm a little ashamed that I never have measured up to what my family wanted me to be. I feel guilty, like I owe my parents a wedding like they want me to have. They won't get to fuss with another wedding, because I'm the only child left since my sister's death.

"I'm trying to take care of my parents' feelings and those of my family and yours. I'm also pressured for time because of my schoolwork, and it's not going to be possible for me to spend a lot of time planning this wedding. It doesn't make any difference to me at all who marries us. But I don't want distance because of this. I get really upset when people fight about religion.

"I'm trying to be the peacemaker: and I'm trying to get you to go along with the church wedding for my parents' sake. It really isn't a big deal to me. My parents are good people who love me a lot and want me to be happy.

"I may be neglecting what I really want because what my parents and you want is so strong. I wonder what I would really like? I honestly don't know."

Part 2 (Philip looks for similarities in their statements).   "We both want a special wedding. We don't want to be hypocrites. We want my family to be happy."

Part 2 (Anne looks for similarities in their statements).   "We are both afraid your family will cut us off financially. We want to get married. We want to have our families and friends there. We want our wedding to be meaningful."

Part 3 (Anne waves her magic wand). "If I could wave my magic wand, your family would understand that I'm not some kind of substitute bride for your sister. They would be respectful of my religious choices. They would be supportive emotionally and financially. Our wedding would be performed by the people who are spiritually important to us. And we'd have the ability to pay for it ourselves."

Part 3 (Philip waves his magic wand). "I guess I really don't know what I want here. I want to marry you, I know that much! I would like to have the ceremony be special, something that reflects who we really are. I don't want to lie. I want my family there. And I want things to be peaceful so that I can focus on my studies. And I want to give my parents what my sister can't give them."

Part 4. Anne and Philip agreed they would need to find a wedding option that was somewhere between what his parents wanted and what Anne wanted. They knew they weren't going to satisfy everyone. As long as both of them were satisfied, that would be enough. They made plans to look for new options by consulting people who might have dealt with similar issues.

Anne's Tarot exercise had brought her to a greater understanding of Philip's parents. Now she agreed to include some Catholic elements in their ceremony, and she suggested having singers perform an old Latin hymn that she loved. Anne said she would make other compromises as long as the marriage itself wasn't performed by a priest. She also wanted to feel free to make choices without financial pressure, and she offered to do some tutoring so they could carry a larger share of the wedding expenses themselves.

Through the Ritual of Listening, Philip realized that he was trying to be all things to all people, and he was giving away his own choices and wants in the process. Through hearing Anne's words, he realized that he wanted to marry her in a way that respected who she was, and that he would have to risk offending his family to do so.

He promised Anne he would think about it, but his studies took up virtually all his time for the next two weeks. The following weekend, he had set aside a day at Anne's request to attend her coven's annual picnic. She suggested that they have breakfast that day with Ed and Jackie, the coven leaders, who had a lot of experience performing weddings. Together, the four of them looked for a solution that would please the engaged couple first, but also honor her faith and his family.

Neither Anne nor Philip wanted to be married in another Christian denomination. A public Wiccan handfasting was also unacceptable, since it failed to respect Philip's choice not to believe in any particular religion.

In the end, they decided on a civil ceremony to be performed by Jackie, in her capacity as a notary. Jackie also brought up a ceremony she had once seen, in which an Episcopal priest gave a "marriage blessing" to a couple after a nonreligious wedding. She wondered if they might be able to find a Catholic priest to do the same. Anne agreed that such a blessing would be an acceptable way of honoring the religion of Philip's upbringing.

They also talked about how to present this choice to Joe and Donna. Philip, who knew his mother loved to feel needed, came up with the idea of asking Donna to find the priest to bless the marriage. Anne asked that they try to pay for the wedding using only their own resources so that his parents couldn't use money to force the couple's decisions. Philip wasn't sure that was necessary, but he agreed it was a good way to take money out of the discussion.

While they'd been talking about ceremonies, Philip had gotten curious. He'd never seen a Wiccan marriage ceremony. Would Ed and Jackie allow him to look at one? He read it over and started asking questions, and the three Wiccans filled him in on their traditions. "This is interesting," Philip said. "I like the ceremony—yes, it talks about the Goddess and God, and I'm not really a believer, but I like the fact that this ceremony doesn't tell you what you should do with your lives. It's too bad we can't do something like this."

"Who says you can't do it?" asked Ed. "We could do it this afternoon if you like. It wouldn't be legal, but it would represent your first formal vows to each other, and I know the others would be delighted to take part."

Anne loved the idea, but only if Philip agreed to it from his own heart, rather than trying to please her. So she kept quiet for a moment, and she was delighted when he said "Really? Let's do that!" Pleased, Ed and Jackie added a few ritual items to their picnic baskets, while Anne and Philip chose crystals to serve in place of rings.

The simple ceremony was performed without special clothing or expense, surrounded by friends and good wishes. Anne was deeply joyful afterward, and Philip felt better knowing they were bound together no matter what.

Their civil wedding a few months later was not the one Joe and Donna would have chosen for their son. It was simple in style, for Anne began by asking Philip to refuse his father's financial aid. When it came down to the decision about how many people to invite, Joe intervened and asked the couple to let him pay for a bigger hall so more of the family could attend, and he was pleased at his "victory" when they said yes. The priest's blessing gave the older couple comfort. Anne and Philip were delighted with the ceremony, but even more delighted to be married to each other.

Myth: The Gruesome Goddess

In the ancient Shinto mythology of Japan, Izanagi was a god and his sister Izanami was a goddess. Together, they were beautiful, powerful, and fruitful. They created all the lands of the earth, then settled in Japan, where they married and began pro-creating. Izanami gave birth to islands, nations, goddesses, and gods, until finally she gave birth to the god of fire. This birth was so painful that she died.

Izanagi was crazy with grief. He traveled to Yomi, the dark underworld, to beg her to return. Alas, she had eaten the food there, and so was forbidden to leave. He defied the laws of the underworld and lit a flame so that he could see his beloved. What he saw was a rotting corpse.

Horrified, he ran away. His wife, furious that he could not accept what she had become, sent demons to kill him, then chased him herself. He barely escaped by rolling a boulder across the doorway to the underworld. Hurling insults at each other from either side of the boulder, they dissolved their mar-riage. The dead and the living have been separated ever since.

This myth speaks to some of the fears we have around hon-esty. If we reveal our true selves to our partners, will they be disgusted with us? Will our partners run away? Will the truth break us apart? Often these fears are ungrounded, but they are still real. The exercises associated with this section, especially the Ritual of Listening, may help you feel safer in telling your truth.

A MOMENT OF TRUTH

In their work on Consensus, George and Vicki (see chapter 2) had made a deal. She would take some specific actions to sup-port his needs for touching and sexual release, and he would take some specific actions to give her free time away from her responsibilities. They had also agreed to check in after four weeks to see if the arrangement was working for them.

They both tried to make it work. George dutifully came home early each Monday night. For a couple of weeks, Vicki reveled in her free time, shopping, seeing friends, and going to the gym, with no kids in tow and no dinner to make. The first time she came home to find George had left the kitchen a mess. But the kids were fed and in bed, and what did it really matter? The second time he met her at the door—her mom needed a prescription picked up, and he couldn't leave the kids. The following week was Parents Night at their children's school, and Vicki didn't get her time off, and the fourth week she couldn't go out because of car trouble. By this time she was starting to feel like "time off" carried too big a price in aggravation.

George, as part of their deal, was supposed to receive back rubs from Vicki, but it was difficult to get her to fulfill this promise. He didn't want to pressure her, and after the first time she didn't initiate the process. She went along with it the one time he suggested a back rub, but it was cut short when young Sophy had a bad dream and started crying in bed.

Vicki didn't have as much trouble giving George time and space for meeting his sexual needs in private. She agreed to his requests for time, taking the children out or keeping them downstairs until he reappeared. She ignored his request for some sign of interest or participation.

They had scheduled another meeting to go over what they had experienced, but Vicki's car had to go in for repairs and they couldn't get the free time till a fifth week had gone by. Vicki was secretly dreading this meeting. She knew she hadn't lived up to her part of the deal, and she was expecting blame and recriminations. The extra week gave Vicki time to think— time in which neither of them performed the actions of their agreement.

During that week, the car broke down again, and she couldn't go to work until the tow truck had come to take it away. The delay was a blessing to her: totally free time, alone, at home, with no chores and no one needing her attention! Vicki spent a couple of hours walking around the garden just reveling in her solitude. It was a beautiful day, and her spirit began to open to the sunlight, the plants, the green earth.

With that time to think, she began to ask herself questions she'd been avoiding for weeks. Vicki acknowledged that solitude was wonderful, far too rare in her busy life as a wife, mother, and business owner. But wasn't this the life she'd wanted and chosen for herself?

When she'd first met George, Vicki had been delighted to be around him, and she was certain she could spend her life with him. Why now was she pushing him away? The agreement wasn't anything major. Surely she could have fulfilled her part of the bargain. A part of her made this rational argument, while at the same time a part of her rebelled, saying "Because I don't want to!"

Vicki recognized that voice. It was the voice of her kids, pushing against some perfectly logical parental directive such as "brush your teeth." In that bright morning, in the solitude of the home she loved, she saw a little more clearly. This wasn't the voice she wanted to use. She wanted to put her adult self back in charge, to do whatever work was required—work which, she suspected, would require more than a few simple exercises. It was time to look inside herself, to find out what the real problem was. George deserved better. And so did she.

In the days after her morning in the garden, Vicki was able to sustain the feeling of strength she had found. She did the Four Points of Perspective exercise (see appendix) as a way of examining who she had become, as opposed to the person she wanted to be:

As Vicki sees herself.   The card indicates weakness and cowardice and a failure to follow through. She recognized that she was weak, and she wondered whether she was being too hard on herself.

As Vicki sees George.   She sometimes felt stifled by George's feelings and desires. She felt like a captive, as if giving in to his wishes would be a form of servitude rather than a gift

or shared pleasure. Deep down, a part of her saw him as an authority figure rather than an equal.

As George sees Vicki.   The 4 of Pentacles reversed, again indicating suspense, delay, and opposition. Through this card, Vicki recognized George's feeling of putting his own progress on hold to make room for her needs.

As George sees himself.   The Lovers reversed, at the most obvious level, indicates he felt like a failure as a lover. Delving a little deeper into the meaning of the card, Vicki found added aspects indicating influences from outside their relationship were getting in the way of George's success in sustaining their passion.

In addition, the predominance of Major Arcana cards in this reading reaffirmed her sense that the issues raised here were important, that this relationship was at a pivotal stage.

Before her morning alone at home, Vicki knew something was wrong in her marriage, and she was trying to make changes for George's sake. What changed? Now she wanted to make changes for her own sake. The way she was acting was not the way she wanted to be. Yet she also realized the power of the emotions that had gotten her into this stalemate. She suggested using the Ritual of Listening to talk about the difficult parts of herself. She also went through the Honesty Questions to prepare. Again, what follows are simply their statements. In each case, they listened to each other's words without interrupting and restated them without judging, until the speaker was satisfied with having been heard.

Part 1 (Vicki states the issue in her words).   "I have to start by saying how hard this is for me to do. I really feel bad that I didn't keep up my end of things this past month. I don't know what happened. I know that sex is a good thing, a gift from the Goddess. And I thought what happened with my brother when I was seven was no big deal anymore. But it keeps coming up again and again. I'm ashamed that I liked the attention from him: I'm ashamed that what he did to me felt good. I'm ashamed that I wasn't a good girl. I somehow feel that if I'd been better behaved, then this would have never happened to me. I got a lot of messages that only bad girls do that kind of thing. And I believed something about me deserved what happened. I didn't want my brother to feel bad about what he did. I didn't want Mom and Dad to know that I was so bad. I didn't want them to get mad at me or him or each other!

"But when I look at our daughter, Sophy, and see how innocent she is at seven, I guess I see that maybe the whole thing wasn't about me, it was about him. Somehow I felt like I owed my brother sexual play after the first time I let him touch me. I feel really dirty, and like I gave away something that was mine because I wanted him to like me and I didn't wish to cause trouble. And afterward I'd pretend nothing ever happened.

"And George, wanting to have sex with me isn't a bad thing, and I know that. But I don't know what is really going on with me. I want you to love me, but I don't want to be sexual with you, or anyone! Half the time I can't sleep, and the other half all I do is sleep! I have to really talk myself into going to work some days. It seems like my work at the store and my work here at the house is never done. My mom drives me nuts every time she calls. Sometimes I just wish the world would go away and leave me alone.

"I want to reconnect with who I am, and to find some way to really work with this thing. I'm afraid that if I cut you off completely that you won't love me. I'm afraid you'll yell at the kids or me and then I'll feel even worse. I'm afraid that I'll dry up and be a bitter old woman like my mother. I'm afraid that I'll find out I really am bad or flawed or dirty."

Part 1 (George states the issue in his words). "I am really angry that you didn't do what you agreed to do. I really went all out to make things work. I feel betrayed by you. I am really feeling like I'm a sucker. But I'm also frustrated and confused, because I didn't do so well either.

"I'm ashamed that I'm not a good lover and father. I used to look at my dad, who was never home, and who yelled at us when he was, and say to myself that I'll never be like that. But I am. I overwork, and when I come home I try to get things to go my way or I get mad or pout. And I yell. I'm doing just exactly what my dad did, and I hate it. My aunt really hated my dad, and she used to tell me I looked like him and that I should be very careful not to be like him. I figured I *was* like him and there was nothing I could do about it. I don't know how to handle it when my feelings get intense, whether they are sexual feelings or jealous feelings or even feelings of love.

"I've been trying really hard to take care of your feelings, Vicki. I want you to be happy and to want to be with me. And I don't, at least on some level, want to try to force you into anything. I feel like it's my job to make you happy. And I hate feeling like I've failed. It reminds me of trying to cheer my mother up after my dad had gone off on one of his yelling jags. I really felt that if I had just been a better kid that my dad would be nicer. So I felt like it was my job to help Mom get over the yelling.

"I really want you to think I'm a nice guy, a sensitive person who cares. And I am. But only sometimes. I'm afraid that I'll be found out to be a fraud, or worse yet, that I am like my dad. I'm afraid that there won't be enough love for me if you go and 'find yourself' somewhere. I'm afraid you'll give your love to someone else. I'm afraid I won't ever have a good sex life."

Part 2 (George looks for similarities in their statements).   "We blew it this last month. We both had some problems with male energy when we were growing up. Yelling scares us both. We sound pretty confused. We both want to be liked. We're both really scared, but we're both interested in making things better between us."

Part 2 (Vicki looks for similarities in their statements).   "I agree with everything you said. And I think we both thought things that happened in our families were our fault. We both wanted to keep things calm. We were way too young to take on what we took on. We brought some stuff into our marriage from what happened to us before, but we both want things to change."

Part 3 (Vicki waves her magic wand).   "If I could wave my magic wand, we would have been born into perfect families! If I could wave my magic wand, I'd get some time and space and help to sort out this thing about my brother, and you would be very understanding and patient. And I wish you would get some help with your temper. And you would know I really do love you."

Part 3 (George waves his magic wand).   "If I could wave my magic wand, you'd be like you used to be and our sex life would be great. If I could wave my magic wand, very nasty things would happen to your brother. We'd find ways to get close to each other, like we used to be. I'd be able to be more understanding. I'd find ways not to let things build up so they come out in yelling. And you'd know I love you, too."

Part 4.   Vicki said she wanted to try counseling to deal with the emotions resurfacing from her childhood abuse. She made an appointment with a therapist and asked George to come with her. They also agreed that the Ritual of Listening helped them to feel both heard and understood. They realized there would be times in the future when they might need to use it again.

The following week, they went to the therapist, who gave them information about support groups for survivors of sexual abuse and their partners. The therapist also recommended that Vicki be evaluated for clinical depression. Vicki agreed to continue seeing the therapist and to try medication to help her establish normal sleep patterns and to see things more clearly.

The initial sessions of counseling were difficult for them. Just making time for the sessions, arranging child care so that they could attend their support groups, was a chore. George stopped going to the partners' group after a few meetings, though it helped him to realize there were others who shared his experience. The medication helped clear away some of the depression that had been keeping Vicki from taking action on her own behalf, and she found in her support group an empowering group of women in various stages of recovery.

Vicki had told George of the healing moment that occurred for her outside in their yard. George thought for a few days about this, looking for a way to help her connect that moment with their marriage. He created the Altar of Healing and Growth (see the Spellbook in the appendix) for them to honor that moment and sustain their marriage through the power of nature.

He shared his ideas with Vicki, and together they set up a pile of stones in a sunlit corner of their yard. For her plant, Vicki chose marigolds for protection. George chose purple impatiens for passion, spirituality, and, well, impatience. They also included their children by taking them to help choose the border and prepare the soil. Tending the plants became a small, pleasant thing that they did together. Amid their hectic lives, it felt good to take a few moments to be quiet and to contemplate flowers and green leaves.

Cynthia Speaks

Especially after Chris had the diagnosis of fourth-stage cancer confirmed, we found it difficult at times to be in genuine emotional communication. Both of us wanted the radiation to isolate and kill the cancer. We had read enough and heard enough about negative thinking that we wanted to do all we could to have a positive outlook. We were tempted to ignore the possibility that the radiation would not work.

We were afraid to name our fears because it seemed that if we did, it would make them real and likely to come to pass. It felt easier to create the impression that things were temporarily difficult, but would get better soon. We tried to ignore the fact that cancer in the fourth stage is not likely to go into remission.

We tried to maintain the illusion of control. We tried to be "perfect" Wiccans, convinced that the Goddess was testing our faith. We each became desperately concerned for the other's feelings, and tried to take care of each other while not taking care of ourselves. We were very afraid of not having the money to pay for medical interventions, of not having the ''right'' information, of not having each other in a body that worked pretty well.

When the radiation did not solve the problem, Chris had a radical neck resection. We hoped that would be the end of it, though it left him scarred. Then, on his birthday the year before he died, the surgeon removed his tongue. Then came the next round of drug therapy—chemotherapy. Again, the medical intervention failed. The cancer had metastasized to his brain and lymph system. His death was just a matter of time.

Over the course of time, we were able—slowly, painfully, haltingly, reluctantly, carefully—to be in contact with our own real selves. I was able to be loving and present for Chris part of the time during the year and a half because I was also able to be angry and tired. He did not have to be cheerful or brave because he could be himself, where he really was. We could be scared together, sad together, happy together.

In the last two weeks of his life, he was hospitalized. Something was dreadfully wrong with the hospital. I had to buy food to give him through his tube because the kitchen kept forgetting to feed him. I brought his medication from home because the on-call doctors wouldn't prescribe methadone and morphine, saying he might get addicted. (He was already addicted: he'd been on those medications for more than a year.) I knew that if he aspirated in the night, no one would be there to help him. So I stayed in the room for several days and nights, leaving only if someone else was there. At best, I was crazy from sleep deprivation and grief.

But I still remember crawling up onto the hospital bed, holding his wasted body, crying and telling him how much I would miss him. He cried with me, and we were more intimate in that moment than we had ever been. Knowing we could still connect on that spiritually deep level, amid the horror of the situation, still touches me in a way that both hurts and heals.

The Work of Honesty

In many ways, the work of establishing and maintaining emotional honesty is the hardest task given to you in this book. If you are in a relationship in which this is not currently a pattern, you may need to start with small steps, first recognizing the behaviors that get in the way of sharing your true self, then slowly working to change them.

Especially if you have old fears and obstructive feelings lurking in your past, you will be tempted to let things lie, to hide your truth and find refuge in codependent patterns.

Ideally, emotional honesty is something that partners can strive for together, helping each other to move away from unproductive patterns and discovering the bonds that come with true sharing. Yet even if you do this work alone, it can be valuable both for your own growth and for your relationship.

CHAPTER 4

Using Your Freedom

The Principle of Giving and Receiving

The North is the area of being grounded, being present in the real world—working, going to school, paying the bills, taking care of your body and your living space. The North is not as much about the past or the future as it is about the present. The work of this chapter is about reclaiming our lives on a moment-by-moment basis. It is about "keeping short accounts," not letting small issues build up to become big problems.

> To honor the North, the place of practical and mundane reality *we both freely give and freely receive.* Neither of us owes the other. What we do, we do because we choose.

It is easier to give freely than to receive freely. We find it much easier to say yes than to say no. Saying "you're welcome" is easier than saying "thank you."

When the Principle of Giving and Receiving is recognized and honored, it looks like this: What we give to one another, we give because we choose to do so. What we receive from one another, we can enjoy without the threat of hidden strings or agendas. There are no IOUs between us.

When I say I will help you, I help you. I do not yell at you while I help you. I do not pretend to help you. I do not criticize you for needing help. I do not resent the fact that I am helping you. I do not remind you for the next six years that I helped you today. And when I need help, I ask you to help me. I do not mope around expecting you to notice that I need help. I respect your right to say no to my request, or to part of it. I appreciate whatever you offer freely. I do not resent that you are helping me. I do not feel I must do something five times more elaborate for you in return.

Chapter 3 discussed codependency, about giving away parts of yourself out of some need to compensate for old hurts. The North reinforces that notion by starting and maintaining a habit of reflecting on ourselves. How am I feeling right now? Not how *should* I feel, but how *do* I feel? Am I excited about the idea of a picnic, or does the notion of potato salad leave me cold? What impact do I seem to be having on the people I'm talking to? What impact are they having on me? What do I need to take care of myself right now? What will fill my spiritual well?

Giving and receiving often take practical, concrete forms. Because of this quality, this is the area where people in relationships often first notice "red flags" when something is out of balance, even when the underlying issue is on a much deeper emotional plane.

What do you have trouble giving? Ruth realized that she was no longer okay with providing child care for Buddy's twice-monthly card game with his friends. She found herself feeling angry and resentful when he left for "boys' night out," and she pretended to be asleep when he got home.

Ruth's own behavior confused her. She had her own night out with her own friends on alternate weeks, and she enjoyed it very much, appreciating Buddy's gift of child care on those nights. For a while, she told herself that she was just being selfish, and that the trade-off was fair.

When she took the time to explore her concerns, staying with the feeling even though it was uncomfortable, Ruth discovered that their lives had changed. As she was doing the laundry, she wrinkled her nose at the stale tobacco smell of the shirt Buddy wore to play cards the night before. The guys used to spend a couple of hours at one friend's house, but lately they had been meeting in a bar, drinking too much for safe driving and leaving Buddy's clothing permeated with cigarette smoke.

Ruth realized that she did not begrudge Buddy time with his friends. Her real objection was to his unsafe driving. When they discussed it, she was afraid of appearing to be petty or controlling, but she needed to tell her truth. Ruth could not freely give Buddy a way to potentially harm himself and others.

What would you like to give? One of the hard parts about freely giving and freely receiving is really believing that "you don't owe me and I don't owe you." Tina's sister Barbara was a successful bond trader, and she often gave Tina and her children lavish gifts. Tina felt bad because Barbara's birthday was coming up and there was no way she could reciprocate.

Tina asked herself: If I had all the money I want, what would I love to get Barbara? The first answers she came up with were "a diamond tiara" and "a trip to Tahiti." She realized that these wishes were her attempt to "make up" for years of financial disparity.

She asked herself again what she would love to give. Some spiritual answers came next: peace, love, happiness. But these were more about Tina's wishes for Barbara than about what Tina would love to give.

The third try was different. Tina remembered how she and her sister had spent hours coloring together as children. She wanted to give that sense of closeness. For Barbara's birthday, Tina wrote a letter describing what she had struggled with, reliving some memories of their growing-up years—and enclosing the biggest box of crayons she could find. This was the first time in years Tina had felt happy about her gift to her sister.

Receiving without guilt: Louie worked nights as a chef, and truly relished his few evenings at home with his partners, Tyler and Eric. They loved having him around, but they felt anxious about cooking dinner for such an expert. Louie occasionally offered to make dinner, and it was wonderful! Tyler and Eric were reluctant to ask him to do so, knowing that he worked hard in a kitchen all week and recognizing that they lacked the skills to return the favor.

Finally Eric brought up the issue. After talking about it, they decided that Tyler and Eric were always free to ask Louie to cook. At the same time, Louie was always free to give or not give. Some nights, they ate stuff out of a can or ordered delivery pizza. But when they got one of Louie's special dinners, they knew he was not resentful, and they felt better able to fully receive the gift and enjoy it.

When Giving Doesn't Help

Many of us have idealistic notions about love and freedom. For people like this, giving is easy. We like to help. We like to share. These kinds of impulses can be a source of trouble when we allow them to outstrip our good sense and willingness to look at how things really are. The following family's experience shows how easy it is to allow a desire to be helpful to mask a deeper problem.

John and Susanna had twin boys who remained in Susanna's custody after their divorce. Several years later, John married Rose. He remained actively involved with his children and paid his child support without fail. Often Susanna would ask for extra money. Usually he gave it to her, figuring the point was to benefit the kids, not to keep a careful accounting of how much "extra" he had done. If he could help the children, he wanted to do it, and money was something he could supply.

Rose agreed that his children were important. Over time, though, it became clear that something was going on that felt really bad to her. Susanna was not a very good budgeter, often needing help in the last half of the month. Susanna seemed to be able to lend money to her friends or take them out to dinner early in the month. She had leased a car newer than the ones either Rose or John drove.

Partway through one month, Rose got a phone call from Susanna, asking for money for gas and food for the kids. Rose and John had just reviewed their own budget, and they had started cutting back on spending so that they could afford to go on vacation together.

Rose immediately felt guilty. "How can I think about spending money on travel when John's kids are hungry and there is no gas in the car? What happens if there is an emergency? How would Susanna get to her job?"

Somehow Rose and John had been infected with the notion that a need constitutes an obligation. It wasn't that they didn't have the money. They did, and they wanted to use it for a vacation. Yet obviously a vacation was less urgent than food for kids. So what to do?

One of the hardest things for John to do was to disentangle himself from the notion that he "should" give Susanna what she asked for if he had it to give. Part of the problem was that he had let Susanna define what and how much he had to give. As he reflected back on their relationship, he realized that he had enjoyed being the white knight to Susanna's damsel-in-distress requests. The idea of saying no to her left him feeling guilty.

First, Rose and John talked about the situation. They

agreed that they could freely give whatever it took to keep the children fed. They also agreed that they could not freely give up their own resources so Susanna could treat her friends to dinner. Both of them wanted to go on vacation and to feel free to enjoy themselves.

They came up with a solution that worked for them. They decided they would no longer give Susanna extra money directly. Instead, they asked her to follow them to a gas station, where they paid for a tank of gas. Then they gave her a coupon from the supermarket redeemable for food. They decided to budget an amount every month to be used for food or gas if Susanna asked.

Susanna had many genuine problems and a lack of material resources. The real issues here were about Susanna's freedom to choose, and whether someone else should pay the cost for those choices. The answer that Rose and John came up with was this: "The children should not pay. And neither should we."

Each of us has the right to enjoy and use our tangible resources—money, time, health, energy, knowledge. Each of us has the right to increase those resources, to change them, and to transform them. Each of us has the responsibility to gather and use resources in an honorable way. By freely giving and freely receiving, we respect others' rights, but also honor our own.

Myth: The Bloody Banquet

Making decisions about giving is fairly straightforward—we weigh our resources, our goals and our situations, then decide what to do. Receiving freely is more difficult, because notions of politeness interfere with the emotional honesty practiced in the previous chapter. This story begins with a gift that's too good to be true, "an offer you can't refuse."

Of all the gods of Egypt, perhaps the best-loved was Osiris.

He ruled the country directly as its divine king, and he had abolished human sacrifice and introduced the arts of agriculture.

Osiris had a brother, Set, who was jealous and violent. Set threw a banquet, invited everyone, and put on a lavish spread to impress the guests. At the end of the evening, as a final gesture of hospitality, Set brought out a beautifully decorated coffin and said he would give it to the guest who fit it best.

This wasn't quite as weird as it sounds. The Egyptians cared deeply about the fate of their bodies and souls after death, and an elaborate coffin was something many people strove for all their lives. The gesture was akin to giving away a new car at the end of a party.

The coffin had been made to fit Osiris perfectly, and as soon as he stepped into it, Set and his servants shut it up tight and tossed it into the Nile.

Osiris's wife Isis found out about this treachery, and she devoted herself to searching for her husband's body. When she finally found it, she hid it in a marsh, but Set found it and ripped it to shreds—a horrible desecration by most standards, but even worse to the Egyptians, who believed the conservation of the physical body was important to achieving afterlife.

By patient searching, Isis was able to find and reassemble almost all of Osiris's body. She then bound up the pieces with linen, and the Egyptians used this story to explain why they mummified their dead. Thanks to Isis, Osiris was able to attain a spirit form, and he continued his royal career as King of the Dead.

The story of Osiris and Isis can be read as a metaphor for putting the pieces of ourselves back together after a traumatic event—a process that can take months, years, or a lifetime.

CENTERING: THE STRENGTH TO GIVE AND RECEIVE

The work of giving and receiving is most difficult when we're not in touch with what we really want and feel. That's why the exercises in this chapter are things you can do by and for yourself, to clarify your own goals and principles. In doing this, you gain the strength needed to say "I'm sorry, it won't work for me to give that" or "Thank you, but I don't feel free to accept that."

In honoring the North, we honor what we have been and done today, acknowledging our gratitude for the gifts granted to us through our world and through others. We make a reasonable and achievable plan for the immediate future so that our efforts will count toward a goal. Where we have violated our ethics or our commitments, we apologize and make amends.

To be present in the moment, to be free to give or receive, means we must make a deep commitment to integrity, striving toward wholeness and wholeheartedness, toward a self that is genuinely intact both inside and out.

We can only give and receive with integrity if we have a foundation of personal strength on which to draw. As chapter 3 noted, we spend a lot of time worrying about what others think about us, trying to read their minds so we will please them. We do this because we think something is missing inside us and we need their approval and praise, or at least their tolerance. We say we need to feel good about ourselves. Some people call this "self-esteem." It's more than that, though. It's a gift of the spirit, available to anyone who is willing to work to achieve it. We call this *centering*.

In Pagan and other paths, *centering* is used to describe a specific ritual act, a meditation or set of actions intended to help the worshiper set aside distractions and everyday problems to focus on spiritual goals. And we describe ourselves as "centered" when we have the spiritual and emotional strength to focus on the truth of the moment and make decisions based on that truth.

Some will say that a lack of centering comes from an unhappy childhood. Some will say that it comes from taking fashion magazines too seriously. Others will say it's because other people put you down. Some say it's a chemical imbalance. Lots of people have made lots of money on these theories.

Centering comes from only one place. It comes from *setting and reaching your own manageable goals.* If you set a goal to brush your teeth tomorrow morning, and you brush your teeth, and you acknowledge that you brushed your teeth, you will move a little closer to your center.

There are three problems most of us have with this idea. First, we have foggy notions about what a goal is. A goal is something that you can count, weigh, measure, time, or capture on videotape. If it isn't that clear, it's not a goal. It has to be something about which you can say, "yes, I have done this" or "no, I have not done this." For instance, if you set the goal of being nice, you'll never reach that goal. *Nice* is too slippery a word, and most of us have a very active inner critic that says we weren't "nice enough." If you set the goal of not yelling at your brother-in-law today, an outside observer can easily tell whether or not you yelled at him. And you will center yourself by not yelling at him if you acknowledge you met your goal.

Second, even if we manage to set concrete goals, we often have a hard time with "manageable." If you set a goal to clean the living room, you will never reach it. You may dust, vacuum, wash the curtains, polish, fluff, and spray all day long. But in the back of your mind, you may believe the room isn't really clean until you repaint it and lay fresh carpet, or you may see your work undone by kids or dogs or the furnace, or you may forget to vacuum under the couch. And therefore the living room is not "clean." If you set a goal to dust the tabletops, vacuum the rug, and clean the TV screen, and you acknowledge that, you'll get three steps closer to your center.

The third part of the problem is that we don't take the time to plan our goals. Most of us lead busy lives, and it takes self-discipline to take two or three minutes to plan, and to acknowledge our successes. The Centering Worksheet (see examples later in this section and a blank one in the appendix) is intended to move you closer to your center by giving you a concrete way to acknowledge your accomplishments and express gratitude for the positive things in your life.

───────────────── *Jane Speaks* ─────────────────

I n religious rituals, I take time to center before beginning. Sometimes, in daily life, I need to take time to center as well. A few moments of quiet contemplation can often help me figure out where I am giving or receiving too much or too little, what my feelings are, and what problem may lay beneath those feelings.

For instance, my husband and I just returned from a long trip that required packing the car full of stuff. When the hours of driving were over and we were finally home, I offered him a gift: Since he had to work the next day and I didn't, I would unpack the car then, and he could have a couple of hours of relaxation that night.

The next day, while I was unloading the car, I began to get very resentful, feeling that he should have offered to help with the unpacking, and even venting a little steam by yelling at his absent self. Realizing that this was irrational—after all, I had offered the gift freely—I walked away from the crowded backseat for a moment to figure out what was really going on.

A few minutes of centering helped me to realize that this had nothing to do with him, and everything to do with me. I was still very tired from the trip, and I was anxious about an important item—my checkbook—that had been lost somewhere in the luggage.

I took care of my immediate need by taking a nap. Refreshed, I returned willingly to my unpacking, and I found the lost checkbook in the glove compartment, right where I'd left it.

───────────────────────────────────

A DAD DIVIDED

Several years ago, Ed had come to terms with the fact that he was gay. This had meant the end of his marriage. Tracy, his ex-wife, had been very angry, and she had restricted Ed's contact with their daughter, Maggie. Ed continued running his home-improvement business, saw his daughter whenever Tracy allowed it, and found love with Rob, a medical transcriptionist. Together Ed and Rob had built a pleasant life: They bought and remodeled an old house in their city, participated in a men's drum circle, and worked for political causes.

Then everything changed. A car accident left Tracy paralyzed, with medical issues that meant she was no longer able to care for her daughter. There was no question in Ed's mind that he would give Maggie a home. He turned their guest room into a third-grader's room and changed his work hours to could spend more time with her.

Rob was sympathetic, but at the same time unhappy. He understood Ed's need to be a father to his child, but did that have to mean becoming a full-time "Uncle Rob"? He hadn't ever wanted children. While he liked Maggie, he resented the time her presence took away from the things he and Ed enjoyed doing together—attending rituals, meetings, and concerts, making love without having to be quiet, sleeping late on weekends.

Rob and Ed talked honestly about what was happening for each of them. They tried various accommodations. Getting a sitter one night a week gave them some valuable time together, but they often spent that time doing household shopping or working out schedules. Taking Maggie along to the Gay Pride rally was a bit of a failure—the girl was scared of crowds, and Ed was furious when her picture was on the TV news.

As Maggie settled in, Ed learned that the city's school system wasn't as safe as he would have liked, nor did it offer the challenges he thought his daughter should have. He began to think about moving to a place with better schools.

Six months after Maggie moved in, Ed came home from work smiling. A former client had called to say she was selling her house, and Ed thought it would be perfect—a nice suburban neighborhood with kids nearby, good schools, a fenced-in yard. He loaded Maggie and Rob into the car to go look at it, and talked nonstop all the way. The visit was filled with Maggie's questions and Ed's careful inspection, and it wasn't until they were on their way home, with Maggie asleep in the backseat, that Ed noticed Rob hadn't said much.

"What's going on?" Ed asked quietly.

"I've got some thinking to do," was all Rob said.

Ed nodded, familiar with Rob's need to process information in his own mind before making decisions. "Is it about the move? Are you okay with this?"

Rob was silent for a moment. "Yeah, I'm okay," he said. His mind wandered back to their house in the city. Sharing that place with Ed had meant a great deal to him. As a gay man in a friendly urban neighborhood, he felt he was less likely to encounter prejudice and ignorance. Moving would change everything. The new neighborhood reminded him of the place he'd grown up—a place where he had been desperately unhappy. He and Ed would have to watch themselves in public. Their lives would revolve around kids' activities.

Over the next month, Rob grew increasingly withdrawn. Moving day was only a few weeks off, and he had barely begun to organize his things. In fact, he'd bought a bunch of new plants for the front porch—saying they would impress prospective buyers—and he spent a great deal of time tending them.

Busy choosing new room colors and working things out with the bank, Ed didn't notice at first that Rob was spending less and less time interacting with him. Finally, though, he realized he needed to make time to find out what was really going on.

"Rob, something's not right," Ed said. "I feel like you're spending more time with those plants than you are with me. You said you were okay with making this move, and I believed you. But I also want you to be happy, and I'm worried about you."

Rob knew he needed to do something. "But I don't know what," he told Ed.

"We promised to give and receive freely," Ed said. "I don't want to receive your gift of moving if it's going to make you miserable. Have you been able to spend any time in meditation, or just centering yourself? That might help you figure out what's going on for you."

Ed offered to do the Centering Worksheets (on the following pages) along with Rob, to try to regain some focus on their relationship. Their busy lives made it tough to remember to do the worksheets, but by reminding each other, they were able to establish the habit. In the third week of the exercise, with the move just two weeks away, they sat down to compare notes, and each brought the previous day's sheet.

DAILY CENTERING WORKSHEET
(Rob)

Today, for my personal care, I need to:

☒ 1. Get hair cut.

☒ 2. Pick up dry cleaning (check hem in gray pants).

☐ 3. Return library books and look for new novel.

Today, for living in general, I need to:

☐ 1. Change address on magazine subscriptions.

☒ 2. Make dinner reservations with Max and Paul.

☒ 3. Feed plants and sweep front porch.

Today, for my work, I need to:

☒ 1. Finish Dr. Bradbury's tapes.

☒ 2. Get started on next batch of work for Med Center.

☒ 3. Finish homework for Continuing Ed class.

Today, for my world, I need to:

☐ 1. **(Family)** Stop at Asian store for soy sauce.

☒ 2. **(Friend)** Call Lana next door and ask about her surgery.

☒ 3. **(World)** Make signs for City Council meeting.

Today I am grateful for these twenty things. Freedom, good health, delicious dinner, Max and Paul's friendship, Lana's recovery, positive feedback from my boss, my hair isn't going gray yet, good neighbors, I think we're going to make a real difference with the City Council, gorgeous new planter, low electric bill, the new Japanese restaurant, great new shoes, good workout, the party last weekend, the beautiful brick sidewalks on our street, I think I'm really doing well in the computer class, I remembered to water the plants, I got the concert tickets, and I get paid tomorrow!

DAILY CENTERING WORKSHEET
(Ed)

Today, for my personal care, I need to:

☒ 1. Go through the two boxes in Maggie's closet and decide what I really want to keep.

☒ 2. Call real estate agent.

☒ 3. Find the mortgage records.

Today, for living in general, I need to:

☒ 1. Get to grocery store (paper towels, cereal).

☒ 2. Get home in time to get cleaned up for parent-teacher meeting.

☐ 3. Remember to water Rob's plants.

Today, for my work, I need to:

☒ 1. Estimate Walton project.

☒ 2. Call supplier about molding for Bergers's porch.

☒ 3. Make arrangements for crew to work without me during the move.

Today, for my world, I need to:

☒ 1. (Family) Call Tracy and give her new phone number.

☒ 2. (Friend) Remind Rob that I really do care about him.

☐ 3. (World) Get water bottles out of Maggie's room and into the recycle bin.

Today I am grateful for these twenty things: Maggie's smile, new house will have a dishwasher, Walton job is coming along nicely, sunny days, nice breeze this afternoon, molding cost less than I budgeted, Maggie liked the school, music teacher seems good, phone call with Tracy didn't go too badly, I found the mortgage papers, Maggie didn't have any nightmares last night, the strength I get from the Gods, my confidence in my ability to make a new home for us, Tracy's survival (so Maggie still has a mom), Rob says Lana's getting over her operation, the taste of good beer after a long day at work, the new ladder's holding up well, two phone messages from prospective clients, Maggie's story that she wrote in class, I remembered to get stuff for breakfast tomorrow.

Comparing their two sheets helped Rob to talk about the differences in their paths. "You're really focused on being this suburban dad, and I'm glad for you, and glad for Maggie that you're able to be there for her. But I don't see a place for me." Confused, Ed assured Rob that there was plenty of room for his plants and hobbies in the new house. But it wasn't about that—it was about feeling at home, and about being his own person rather than Maggie's second dad.

Rob had gained some strength from the centering exercise, and it helped him say the difficult words. He told Ed, "I love you, and I want you to be happy as a man and a father. I always want to be your friend. But I don't feel I can go with you."

Ed had worked hard to build and sustain this relationship. He was hurt and disappointed, but not really surprised. He had felt the increasing distance, and he understood that if he had to choose, he would have to choose Maggie. These days, Ed realized, he almost didn't have room in his life for a partner—at least, for a partner who wasn't an enthusiastic parent.

"I don't want to lose you, but maybe that's the price I have to pay," he said. "I love you and want to be your friend, too, and I appreciate your honesty. I'm sad about ending what we have, but Maggie needs me more right now. Let's think about how to do this in a peaceful and respectful way."

They made plans to separate, not without regret, but realizing that they'd both done what they could do. They settled some practical matters—Rob was going to get a roommate and buy out Ed's share of the city house—but the decision left them both feeling uncertain about the future. As a way of reassuring each other, they used the centering Tarot spread (see appendix). First Rob read for Ed:

Interpretation.   Ed has a lot of demands on his energy but is staying on top of them so far. He resents the stress and conflicts the situation is causing in his life, but he is grateful for the practical daily matters that keep him from living too much in the difficult world of emotions. The advice here is to see things as they are and to take action rather than waiting for a ship to come in. He fears threats and nastiness, whether from Rob or from his ex-wife, and he seeks a situation where there will be fewer demands on him. Here the advice is to trust only himself, and choose the path that is right for him without allowing others to lead him.

With this reading, Ed saw that his immediate road ahead would be difficult (hence the high number of reversed cards). Yet at the center, there was himself, strong and victorious, able to maintain a position of stability. He resolved to spend extra time building connections in the new town for himself and Maggie, and to do everything in his power to avoid making the separation from Rob any more difficult than it had to be.

The reading for Rob had a different tone:

Interpretation.   Rob's primary feeling is that of loss. He does not blame the innocent Maggie (indicated by the child on the Sun card). Indeed, he likes her and values her youthful vitality. Yet he resents the dramatic changes in the life he loved, and he cannot help but feel liberated at the thought of leaving the situation behind.

The reversed Hanged Man indicates decisive action. Rob is afraid of acting too hastily, of giving up the certainty and commitment he had with Ed, yet he sees that it is possible to effect the separation without violent upheavals, to do this in a civilized way. The advice points toward a new beginning, particularly one focused on business or career.

This reading confirmed some of what Rob already knew, and it also brought up some issues he hadn't thought that

much about, such as the feeling of freedom at the thought of a life without a child in the house. In talking about the message of the cards, he and Ed reaffirmed that they wanted a minimum of unpleasantness, and that they wanted to remain friends. As a gesture of friendship, Rob gave Ed one of his beloved plants for the new house.

Rob and Ed had undergone a formal handfasting ritual early in their relationship, and they decided it was now important to separate spiritually as well as physically and emotionally. They asked a Wiccan friend to officiate at their handparting ritual (see appendix), which is appropriate as a semiprivate rite for a couple parting on civil terms. Besides freeing them on the spiritual level, this ritual let them affirm their desire to part without rancor, and to promise not to speak ill of each other.

Myth: The Serpent Husband

In India, long ago, a priest found his wife weeping because she could not bear a child. "Dear one, stop your grieving," he said. He had just come from offering a sacrifice for the birth of a son, and an invisible voice had said their son would be handsome, virtuous, and blessed with good fortune. As predicted, his wife soon became pregnant. Imagine their surprise, then, when his wife gave birth not to a boy, but to a snake!

Ignoring the advice of others to get rid of the snake, the mother gave her son a large, clean container to live in, fresh milk and food, and cared for him as he grew. One day, she witnessed the wedding procession of a neighbor's son, and she began crying, accusing her husband of failing to arrange a marriage for her child. Her husband tried to point out that no respectable girl would marry a snake, but his wife's face was so sad and his love for her so great that he promised to try.

He went to see a friend in a faraway city, mentioning that he was seeking a wife for his son, but not mentioning the son's unusual shape. "Seek no further!" said his friend. "I have a daughter whom I would be honored to give you." And so the marriage was arranged, as was the custom in that time and place.

When the bride was brought to her new home, her attendants heard townspeople muttering about what a shame it was that such a beautiful girl should be married to a snake. They urged her to call off the wedding, but she refused, saying "Not even wise men and gods can resist the decrees of fate." Besides, she said, she did not want to dishonor her father by breaking the engagement.

The girl and the snake were married, and she acted considerately toward him, keeping him in a large basket in her bedroom and bringing him milk and food. One night, the snake left his basket, assumed the form of a man, and got into bed with his wife. Not recognizing him, she screamed and ran to the door before hearing his cry, "I am your husband!" To prove it, he transformed himself back into a snake, then to a man again. The prophecy made before his birth was fulfilled, for he was handsome and virtuous, brought to his true form through love.

Here, then, is the mystery of giving and receiving: To give love freely, we must accept our partners as they are, and give to the imperfect person before us without expecting those imperfections to change. Yet through giving and receiving, through the daily give-and-take that builds our lives, it is possible to experience the gifts and acceptance of another as a transforming force, to see the imperfections fully and yet give one's love with the radiant joy of a fairy-tale romance.

THE GIFT OF TIME

Getting help in dealing with her past was doing wonders for Vicki. Over a few months, her therapy and her support group had become sources of refuge and strength, and she was experiencing good results from her medication. She began working through some old issues, taking such small steps as setting boundaries on her mother's phone calls.

She felt happier, more alive. Yet she was not yet ready to feel sexual, as her husband George so ardently wished she would. He, meanwhile, was tired of struggling to keep ahead at work while struggling to make things better at home. The tension between them had affected their children, who needed extra attention and reassurance from both parents.

One evening, Vicki came home from her support-group meeting glowing. The group was planning a weekend retreat, and she really wanted to go. She asked George to think about whether this would be okay with him.

As they discussed it, they discovered several issues. First, if Vicki went away, George would be responsible for all child care and housework on that weekend. Second, it would cost money. Finally, it would mean Vicki would miss the annual company outing for George's firm.

George was happy that Vicki had found solace in the group and that she felt comfortable there as she worked to heal. He was also a little sad that she couldn't seem to find that solace with him. Thinking about her request, he realized he could freely give her the time spent on housework and child care— after all, he wanted to do more with the kids anyway. He could freely agree to her spending the money.

What George did not feel free to give up was having Vicki at the company outing. His job was important to him, and he counted on Vicki's presence, skills, and charm to help bolster his image with bosses, coworkers, and clients.

As they talked, Vicki realized there was a part of this package that she did not feel comfortable receiving freely. She was fine with the money, and she had never enjoyed the company outings anyway. Yet she did feel guilty about leaving him stuck with the kids and the housework all weekend. This discomfort came out in the form of repeated offers to do some of the housecleaning ahead of time, to arrange for a sitter—things George hadn't asked for and didn't need.

They realized they were defeating themselves before they even got to the point of communicating with each other. Vicki urged George to try the Inner Obstacles exercise (see appendix), which her support group had done together at a recent meeting. They sat together in the living room after the children were in bed and worked through the exercise separately, then shared their results with each other.

George began with this statement:

"I, George, am a loving and lovable husband." His inner critic surfaced immediately: *But your wife doesn't really appreciate you.*

He countered that with:

"I do the very best I can to be a good husband."

Then he tried again:

"I, George, am a loving and lovable husband." *But not such a great lover.*

"That's not all about me. Vicki is a part of this and she thought I was the most wonderful lover when we got married."

"I, George, am a loving and lovable husband." *If you were a really good husband, your wife would be happy and really love you.*

"Vicki does love me, and I didn't make her unhappy."

After thinking about it for a little while, George realized that his statement about himself wasn't what he really wanted to say. *I'm more than my relationship with Vicki,* he thought. So he tried again with a slightly altered statement:

"I, George, am a loving and lovable person." *You aren't that great a person. You aren't very considerate.*

"I am often considerate of myself and others."

"I, George, am a loving and lovable person." *That won't put food on the table.*
"I have a good job, and I do it well. I meet my responsibilities."

"I, George, am a loving and lovable person." *Who isn't getting any.*
"My sex life has nothing to do with my worth as a person."

Hearing the words of his inner critic, George realized he had not truly given Vicki the freedom to heal without pressure to be sexual with him. Even though he had stopped asking for the attention he wanted, deep inside he didn't truly believe he was a worthwhile person unless he was getting that attention. George decided to write the last sentence of his inner dialogue—"My sex life has nothing to do with my worth as a person."—a few more times and meditate on it.

Vicki chose this sentence to represent herself:

"I, Vicki, am a whole and worthwhile woman." *Your brother made you dirty.*
"I am clean, and no one, especially my brother, has the power to dishonor me."

"I, Vicki, am a whole and worthwhile woman." *But you aren't a loving wife.*
"My sexuality is only a part of me. My value and my love are not tied to my willingness to have sex."

"I, Vicki, am a whole and worthwhile woman." *You don't care about your family. You are selfish.*
"I take responsibility for taking care of myself."

Together, George and Vicki talked about their struggles with this exercise. They even made suggestions to help each other better counteract their inner critics. Doing this helped them draw on the knowledge of each other that comes with a long shared life, for each knew what words might mean the most to the other.

As they ended the exercise, George thanked Vicki. "For what?" she asked. "I wanted to do this exercise and you probably would have preferred to be watching TV or reading a book."

George explained that he had felt left out of the growth and happiness she was finding in her support group. In bringing home this exercise from the group and doing it with him, she was giving him the gift of sharing herself and her progress. "I'm not going to deny that the past few months have been very tough for me," he said. "I want you to be happy, even if that means spending some time away from me, but I do want to feel like I'm still part of your life."

George and Vicki turned to the Centering Tarot Spread as a way of helping them decide what to do about her plan to spend a weekend away. First, they did this reading for Vicki:

Interpretation.   Vicki is struggling to set realistic goals and honor herself for her achievements. She also experiences George as sometimes uncooperative. She resents the past, both the abuse that tainted her childhood and the former sexually active partnership that is so vivid in George's memories. Vicki is grateful for the chance to change things in herself and her family, to give her daughter a more protected childhood than she had, and she appreciates the stability George has given her by promising to stay in the marriage while she works to heal.

Vicki fears conflicts that could destroy her home and family, and the advice indicates a retreat from the daily round as a way of moving toward the strength she desires and needs.

This reading confirmed Vicki's sense that the support-group weekend was important in her healing process, and that

it was worth making some sacrifices to attend. The reading also reminded her to freely accept and appreciate George's gifts of sticking by her and working with her, of valuing stability for their children.

George's reading made him think hard:

Interpretation. George's self is represented by the 9 of Pentacles, a card of self-sufficiency, reminding him that he has the power to meet all his own needs, and he does not have to rely on Vicki or anyone else to do so. George resents the back-to-school aspect of the work they are doing together, and he appreciates the spiritual side of his life. The reversed 3 of Pentacles reminds him to focus on the parts of his work that yield the greatest rewards, and to look at the ways his attitude toward work is blocking him from growth and spirituality.

He fears that his resentments and opinions are getting in the way of building the life he wants, a life in which he is the master of himself, respected by others, and able to provide benefits to those he loves. The advice is to direct his energies away from momentary satisfactions toward the greater good.

Based on this reading, George changed his mind about the importance of his company outing. He could now freely give Vicki the gift of her weekend away. The reading reminded him that he needed to rebalance his priorities, to return to the source of his spiritual energy. For George, this meant spending less energy on trying to be successful and more time in nature, which was the source of his spirituality. Vicki saw how happily he began making plans to take the children to a botanical garden. Seeing his delight made it easier for her to let go of her guilt over leaving him alone.

Having come to these decisions, they knew that the work of freely giving and freely receiving would continue to be difficult for them. George had taken to heart the message of the Tarot reading, which encouraged him to rebalance his life, and he realized his spirituality was one area he had been neglecting.

He asked Vicki if she would be willing to participate in a ritual to empower some special herbal incense, to scent their home and fill it with energies they needed.

She agreed, and the next night he brought her a small bottle with a mixture of leaves and petals, ground into small pieces and labeled "Giving and Receiving Incense" (see appendix for recipe). George explained that he'd ground dandelion fluff into the mixture because dandelions that were seeding were the "magic wands" of his childhood—he'd pick the dandelion, make a wish on it, and blow his wish into the wind on the seeds.

Charmed by this description, Vicki placed some of the mixture in a potpourri pot and lit a small candle beneath it. To the incense, they each added a drop of their personal essential oil. As the scent very gently pervaded their living room, George and Vicki stood near the pot, closing their eyes while they did a Centering Meditation (see appendix), repeating the steps back and forth to each other. Both emerged from the ritual feeling calmer and more open to each other.

Cynthia Speaks

In my marriage to Chris, we promised to follow all the Principles described in this book. During Chris's long illness, all these vows were difficult to keep. This vow—promising to freely give and freely receive—was the one that kept us together. If I could not freely give my time, energy, life, or love to Chris, I had to ask for help from others or say no.

Some of the most emotionally wrenching times were the emergency trips to the hospital. We often ended up sitting in the waiting room for what seemed like days, or waiting in the little cubicles for a doctor to see him. The doctors in the emergency room were often medical students, interns, or residents. His last trip to the emergency room was long, irritating, and fraught with misunderstandings as well as a brand-new crop of ER personnel.

Chris was well over six feet tall, and as the cancer progressed, he became less and less able to take care of his own body—a body I was ill-equipped to manage. I am a bit over five feet tall, have had broken bones in my back for years, was seriously depressed, and was on my last reserves of strength. Problems ranged from having only one bathroom on the second floor to coping with his medications and apparatus. I was physically, emotionally, and spiritually unable to care for him any more.

When the medical staff had done what they felt was necessary to stabilize him, they prepared to discharge him. I knew I could not care for him at home. I told him that I loved him, wanted to be with him, and would be there for him as much as I could. I knew he hated hospitals as much as I hated having him in one. But I could not take him home. In front of him, I told the medical staff that I refused to take him home.

They were neither understanding nor compassionate, condemning me as an unloving wife for not caring enough to put myself out for him. It was not the time nor the place to explain the principles of relationship. Chris supported my decision and refused to go home. Through this we held hands.

When they finally transferred him to the oncology floor, I stayed with him. And I felt just terrible. What if I could have done just a little more? I had done all I could freely do, and Chris knew that. And he could not freely receive what I could not freely give. After all, we had promised this to each other.

The Best Gift of All

When we are centered, we are also able to assess our own emotions, to give and receive with an open heart. As you become more adept at giving and receiving freely, you may surprise your partners and friends, especially if they are used to perceiving you as especially compliant or independent. Once they get used to you, however, you'll find your relationships freer, less weighed down by guilt and resentment.

This lightness of heart is a freedom all its own—one that you may recognize from those moments when you've been able to give and receive with your true self. The work of instilling it into your everyday interactions is valuable even if your partner is unresponsive, for it makes you a stronger and happier person.

This skill in particular can be beneficial to your spiritual as well as emotional life. However you perceive the Divine—one Goddess? many Gods? numinous spirits of Nature?—your relationship with divinity is one of giving and receiving. Only you can decide what freely giving and freely receiving means to you in that relationship. Yet considering your spiritual beliefs in these terms may provide an interesting new perspective to inform your worship.

The following chapter will help you to learn more about strengthening your spirit as a way to strengthen your relationship.

Choosing One Another Every Day

The Principle of Balance

Throughout this book, we have emphasized how important it is to be in touch with our true selves as we try to build better relationships with our partners. This chapter emphasizes an equally important relationship: the connection to divinity. We believe this connection—whether it takes the form of a complex ritual practice, regular religious attendance, or an occasional feeling of "something out there"—is essential to living the fullest and most joyful life. We call this connection "spirituality."

Spirituality is not an easy topic to discuss. Some of us cannot find words to describe the experiences we call spiritual. Others are unsure whether what we experience is spiritual, or choose to rely on a guiding principle rather than any divine being. Some have a well-developed sense of what spirituality means for us, and are not interested in increasing our breadth of knowledge, only our depth. Some may be continuing traditions that resonate through time in a family or culture. Others may be seeking and testing, or devising new spiritual expressions.

Spirituality helps us to make decisions about our lives. Our spirituality helps us to become more whole as people, and allows us to make some sense of a confusing world.

> To honor the Spirit, the Center, the place of the Divine, **we choose balance.** We choose how our relationship will balance with the other aspects of our lives. We consider how much time, energy, and resources we are willing to invest in one another. We balance all the Principles against one another, finding ways to be loving while being honest, to give and receive freely while maintaining equality and consensus.

The Principles we have discussed so far tend toward the practical. They look at the present moment, and at the past, and they work together very well.

When we apply them, we find ourselves asking questions. What happens when one principle conflicts with another? How do we prioritize our commitments? How do we incorporate the future, the big picture, into our decisions? What happens when we can't meet the promise we made in consensus to cook dinner every other night? What happens when one partner takes up most of a couple's time and energy every day with emotional honesty about her crummy job or his struggles with parenting? What happens when we find ourselves simply exhausted, depressed, or drained? Here is where the Principle of Balance comes in.

There's no cut-and-dried solution, for the answers are different for every person and every relationship. This chapter will present some ways to think about our visions, our spirits, and our own sense of balance.

Following is one simple place to start: If we imagine our time as a pie, we can visualize cutting the piece that represents how much we give to a certain area. You might spend a third of your time on sleep and personal grooming, another third on work, and all but a tiny sliver of the rest on children and friends. The small size of the sliver for your partner may be a problem, and you may find that very little of your time goes to other things (creativity, exercise, spirituality, learning) that are important to you. How we choose to spend our time, energy, and resources will tell us clearly where we are out of balance.

A Question of Ethics

Many Pagans follow the Wiccan Rede and the Rule of Three as ethical guidelines. (Those who do not do so usually base their ethical rules on ancient history or law.) The Rede, from an Old English word meaning "advise," says: "If it harm none, do as you will." Harm no one and you can do as you please. Clear. Right? If only it were clear and simple! The questions are many: What is "harm"? Who is "none"? Is harm contained in the motivation? In the action? By a deliberate act, or by a failure to act? What about consequences we cannot foresee? What about your notion of harm versus my notion of harm? Does "none" include oneself? Does "none" include the planet, the cow that gives milk or meat, the tree that provides wood to keep a child warm?

One helpful way to consider the Rede is looking at your own responsibility as an expanding circle, with the Divine and yourself at the center. Harming yourself and harming the Divine are the strongest ways you can violate the Rede. Christians have a similar guide: "Love the Lord your God with all of your heart and mind and soul and strength and love your neighbor as yourself" (Luke 10:27). The order is clearly self before others. This is a part of the Principle of Balance.

Are people who follow this Rede self-centered? It's more accurate to call them "self-centering." Self-centering people see to our own needs first and thus respect the Divine, the God and/or Goddess within us. We preserve our lives, our health and our sanity. In taking the best possible care of these personal resources, we preserve them not only for ourselves, but for our families (biological or chosen), our communities and our world. Until we take care of ourselves, we can't give our best energy to those around us.

When we see a person who is "self-centered" in the popular sense of the term, acting as if every event were about him or her, we see someone who is off balance. "Self-centered" people may be described as feeling entitled, demanding to be top priority for others, acting as if they are always the most important, and violating others' boundaries whenever those boundaries are inconvenient. A primarily self-centered individual is simply not trustworthy or respectful.

Self-centering people are aware of their personal responsibility first for themselves, and then for their actions and their impact. A primarily self-centering individual is trustworthy and respectful. Real centering, which we learned about in chapter 4, is the only way we can consistently give our energies to others.

There are times when priorities are difficult to see clearly. Luckily we have the Rule of Three: That which you send out comes back to you threefold. You may choose not to believe it literally, but it offers a thought-provoking way to consider your actions.

If what you do or choose affects others, would you be willing for it to be returned to you three times over? If you dye your hair bright aqua and offend your mother, are you willing to be offended three times over by her choices in superficial matters? If you pump six bullets into an intruder who threatens you in your home, are you willing to have the same returned to you threefold if you threaten someone else in his or her home? If you speak ill of someone who disagrees with your politics, are you willing to have your opponents say three times as many unpleasant things about you?

Living in the real world with an ethical stance is a challenge. It forces thoughtful people to make difficult choices, to choose what their purpose is and how they go about carrying that out. By setting goals to go along with your ethical system, you create another, more personal measuring stick as a check for yourself.

Let's say you set a goal of being debt-free. You can choose to achieve this in a number of ways: robbing a bank, declaring bankruptcy, taking on an extra job, cutting your spending, going back to school for more marketable skills, buying lottery tickets, or doing prosperity spells.

If you bring in the Rede and the Rule of Three, it is easy to discard robbery, which harms the bank and its customers by taking money that belongs to them. The threefold return of this action would suggest that you'd lose your own money three times over. Since bankruptcy harms your creditors by denying them money you legitimately owe them, you will probably choose this only if you have no other options.

Next, you would look at what having an extra job—or going back to school, buying lottery tickets, curtailing spending, or doing that money spell—would mean for your health, sanity, and resources. Then expand your inquiry into the consequences to encompass your family, your community, and your world. After careful consideration, you make a choice and accept the threefold return associated with it. You might choose one or more ways to reduce your debt. Or you might decide the cost of attaining this goal is too high for you, and choose not to pursue it now.

The Rede and the Rule are applications of the Principle of Balance. They encourage you to look at situations in perspective. You can choose many other ethical rules as alternatives, and part of honoring your own connection with the Divine is to recognize and apply your own ethics.

Myth: The Buffalo Dance

The storytellers of Montana's Blackfoot tribe offer this story of balance, of an exchange of energy:

The tribe at one time got much of its food and clothing from buffalo. The easiest way to kill many buffalo at once was to lure the herd over the edge of a cliff, where many would die on the sharp rocks below.

At one point, though, the buffalo became wise to this ruse. The medicine man in his buffalo skin, the men waving their robes, all failed to entice the buffalo to the cliff's edge. The tribe was beginning to go hungry when a young woman, fetching water from the bottom of the cliff, saw the buffalo herd standing on the land above. She called out to them, "Oh, if only you would jump off that cliff, I would marry one of you!"

Remember the saying about being careful what you wish for? The buffalo jumped off the cliff, and one large male buffalo, emerging unharmed from the slaughter on the rocks, leaped up to the young woman and carried her off. Startled, she resisted, but the buffalo reminded her of what she had said and showed her that the buffalo herd had provided plenty of meat for her people.

Delighted at their unexpected good fortune, the people of the tribe were too busy butchering and cooking the buffalo meat to miss the girl at first. When they noticed she was gone, her father resolved to search the land for her.

He traveled many miles until he came to a buffalo wallow, a pond where the herd would rest and drink. Tired and thirsty himself, he sat down beside it and spoke with a magpie nearby. He praised the bird's beauty and added, "If you see my daughter anywhere, tell her 'Your father is waiting by the wallow.'"

The magpie flew up and spotted the girl in the middle of the herd of buffalo and managed to slip the message to her without the bull-husband's noticing. She came to meet her father, but refused to go back with him, saying the herd would follow her and kill her people.

When she returned, her husband sniffed the air and said "I smell a man nearby." She tried to deny it, but the buffalo stampeded anyway, trampling her father into tiny bits. When she wept for her father, her husband said, "Now you know how it is for us, when we see your people kill so many of our number." He offered the tearful girl a deal: She could go home if she could bring her father back to life.

The girl asked the helpful magpie to scour the ground for a piece, no matter how small, of her father's body. The bird brought her a joint from his backbone, and she covered it with her robe and sang a certain song. Slowly, under the cloth, her father resumed his shape, then began breathing, then finally stood up.

The buffalo marveled at her magic, but they also had some of their own to teach: Slowly, solemnly, they performed their own dance and song, and then they instructed the people to perform this buffalo dance whenever buffalo were killed, to restore the spirits of the animals that had died.

AN ETHICAL BASIS FOR SPIRITUALITY

The story of the buffalo dance is about recognizing and honoring the spirit of another. People often question their own spiritual nature, and balancing spiritual life and the practical world may seem confusing. These guidelines for ethical Pagans may help in making real-world decisions:

We each have a right to believe in, serve, and enjoy the Divine in whatever form or forms we find meaningful. A formal ritual in a building may not hold great interest for us, but we can respect that others find this important. Thus if you attend a ceremony in another faith, you try to listen with respect and participate when it is appropriate to do so.

If others serve the Divine by walking door to door to talk

about their faith, you are not required to listen to them. (After all, they are asking for your time, which you have a right to give or withhold in keeping with your own goals and needs.) But their expression of faith, no matter how silly you find it, has as much validity as yours, so you need to respectfully refuse or accept their offer.

Respect for others' spirituality is most vital with the people closest to us. It is an act of love and trust to share your spiritual outlook with your partner, to respect the way he or she understands the Divine, however much that understanding may differ from yours. Many partners find it rewarding to share their spiritual ideas and struggles, learning more about themselves and each other while honoring their differences.

We are free to seek and receive comfort, support, empowerment, and guidance directly from the Source. If the gods tell someone to ask for your money, you don't have to respect that person's statement as spiritual truth. You have the right to check it out directly through your own sources of spiritual information, which might include books, rituals, meditation, prayer, or intuition. Some traditions place far less emphasis on this aspect of receiving spiritual guidance directly from the Source, but even they acknowledge that it is the Divine who acts, with the humans in between as channels or interpreters.

Along with this right to seek our own information, we have the responsibility to accept the consequences of whatever we choose as a result of that seeking. We have the responsibility to encourage others to seek their own relationship with the Divine rather than setting ourselves up as substitutes.

In relationships, this means no partner is considered to be spiritually superior. One may be better trained, more experienced, or have more skill in some areas related to spirituality, but all are equal in terms of their access to divine information, guidance, and inspiration.

We can be as open as we choose about our spirituality, seeking and finding meaningful and enjoyable ways to express it in any area of our lives. This is important, yet can seem difficult if our spirituality is different from that of those around us.

Expressing your spirituality doesn't mean you have to tell everyone you meet about your religion. If one form of expression is uncomfortable or risky for you, you always can choose others. Your expression may be lighting a candle to help you focus on the beauty of the world, or it may be listening to inspiring music and singing along, or walking through an art museum. What's important is that your spirit be expressed and not stifled. The more regularly you offer this expression, the more regularly you are filled.

How does this apply to relationships? You have the responsibility to use that openness and expression to bring helpful change to yourself and others. You have the responsibility not to use your freedom as a means to control or dominate others. You have the responsibility to respect others' choices in expressing their own spirit, as long as those choices do no harm to you or others.

You can believe in, serve, and enjoy the Divine in whatever form or forms you find meaningful. If you find comfort and help in the image of God as an old woman sitting on a porch shelling beans, with all the time in the world to talk to you, then that is a fine thing. If you seek to live that belief, perhaps by trying to offer time to others who need a listening ear, then that is also a fine thing.

What are the Rules?

One of the most important parts of keeping balance in a relationship is agreeing on its structure and ground rules. For some, this may include defining shared goals or underlying assumptions about its duration. Continuing the theme of taking our bodies seriously, we now turn to an element that distinguishes romantic relationships from other types: sexuality.

Those just starting a relationship often assume they know

what form it's going to take—an assumption that may lead to misunderstandings later. Consciously choosing the form of a relationship gives it a much firmer foundation. This act balances all the Principles: Each of you has an equal right to have your needs met within the relationship, and an equal responsibility for putting energy into it. The form of a relationship must be chosen in consensus if it is to stand. To make a choice you can live with, it is vital to be honest with yourself and others about your emotions. Any choice means giving a gift to your partner—whether it be independence, veto power, or your exclusive attentions—and receiving a gift in return.

Because Pagan religions specifically identify sexuality as a sacred part of our lives, many Pagan relationships also include a definition of how the people involved will behave around sexuality in a ritual context.

The most conventional structure is "exclusive" or "monogamous," in which two partners agree to behave sexually only with each other. In some Pagan groups, partners make an exception to exclusivity for the purpose of ritual sexuality. Questions to answer might include: Does our relationship exclude hugs or kisses except to family members? What about phone sex, pornography, or Internet flirtations? Is it okay to raise ritual energy using sexuality if more than the two of us are there? The boundaries will be different in every relationship.

"Polyamory" is a generic term used to describe relationships that involve more than two people. The parameters need to be clear and acceptable to all concerned. This might include answering questions such as: Who sleeps where? Do partners have "veto power" over one another's lovers? Are there times when you agree not to take new lovers?

There are many ways to structure this type of relationship. Often, a central individual or couple provides the focus. Some couples take each other as "primary" partners, giving each other first importance while admitting the possibility of other partners under certain circumstances.

Another variant is "polyfidelity," in which a group of three or more people agree to keep their sexual and romantic relations within the group. Finally, in "open" relationships, partners are free to engage in sexual activity outside the relationship.

One sexual structure that people sometimes overlook is celibacy, in which an individual does not engage in sexual activity with others. This choice—which is one variant of primary with oneself—may come about by choice or by circumstance.

Whether or not you choose to abstain from sexual relations, being primary to yourself can be an empowering and healing experience. One way to implement this choice is to assume that certain levels of sensual contact with anyone else are "always new." This means that each contact, even with a person you've loved before, is weighed and chosen afresh, with the clear understanding that your balance point is within yourself.

Pagans believe none of these forms is wrong, provided they are practiced ethically, with commonsense precautions against disease and unwanted pregnancy. None of these systems is an excuse for "cheating"—breaking promises, endangering others, or lying about your feelings and actions.

When you choose a conventional (heterosexual, monogamous) relationship, the boundaries are more firmly established by society before you begin. If you choose a more complex relationship structure, less likely to be understood and supported by the world around you, everyone involved must work harder at honesty, communication, and listening. This is not necessarily a bad thing! Doing this work can prevent many problems over time, and many partners who thought they didn't need to do it find themselves regretting it later.

When we seek balance, defining our most intimate physical contact is a necessary part of respecting our bodies as sacred. Each person, each couple, each group decides for themselves how they can best express the sacred aspect of their relationship.

Exhaustion and the Vampire

As much as we would like to live in a state of constant spiritual renewal, the world is full of distractions, chores, and tensions. When we commit to following the Principles, we find ourselves taking on a lot of work. We spend time in active thinking, and we must sometimes struggle to communicate with those we love.

The two things most likely to derail our good intentions to live in balance are:

- failing to listen to our anger
- the presence of "vampiric" relationships

We'll talk more about anger later in this section, but for now, let's look at vampires. Vampiric relationships are ones that violate the Principles, often in a very subtle way. When you become aware that one of the Principles is not operating in a relationship, it's also a clue that a problem may exist with balance.

Psychologist Carl Jung believed that when a story is told all over the world, it is because there is a common human experience being expressed. One such story is the story of vampires. From Australia to Africa, from the Pacific Northwest to the Amazon, people have told stories about beings that drain their victims of life, whether physical or spiritual.

From these stories we can draw two ideas for observing our world: First, there are people out there who are seeking and finding life by preying on others. Second, there are people out there who are being preyed upon.

We have all had the experience of being with someone for a time and finding ourselves drained afterward. We might ask ourselves, "Am I just tired? Am I just being selfish? Or is there something else?" If that happens once in a while, it may just be fatigue or stress. If someone evokes this response consistently, though, something else may be going on.

A qualitative and quantitative difference exists between healthy caring and vampirism. There are times in everyone's life when we are in need, and "life"—love, caring, support, and hope—can be fed into our parched spirits through the kindness and presence of others. This is not vampirism, codependence, or any other unhealthy thing. It is compassion and the embodiment of love. And may there be a great deal more of it!

Before you decide that you or someone else is behaving like a "vampire" or "prey," please know that we all have the capacity to play either part, no matter how much we would like to avoid doing so. Indeed, we are likely to take both parts at different times—sometimes even in the same relationship. Vampirism can occur in many kinds of relationships, though many vampires prefer to be romantically and sexually involved with their prey.

A "vampire" is someone who feeds on our life force, our energy, our time, and our resources while giving false hopes of acceptance, praise, or power. Vampires and their "prey" are often not conscious of what is going on. However, we can recognize the potential of a vampiric relationship by noticing how we consistently feel, how we respond, and how we are after the interactions. This is not about you and I giving and taking: It is about one of us giving and one taking as an ongoing pattern.

Look at the following example:

Amy and Carrie were friends, and Amy was going through a rough time. Her boyfriend dumped her, her car broke down, and her job wasn't going well. For a couple of weeks, Amy's life seemed to be one crisis after the other, and Carrie made extra time for her friend, listening with concern.

Things seemed to calm down, but over the next few months, it felt to Carrie as if Amy's problems were all that she and her friend ever talked about. They didn't seem to laugh or have fun together, and after a time Carrie came to dread the telephone ringing because it might be Amy with another sad story. Carrie felt bad for not wanting to be a better friend to Amy, but she found herself feeling empty and frustrated after each encounter, and she noticed that this friendship didn't seem to have room for her own worries and joys.

Vampires and prey are cut from the same cloth: Both are afraid of death or diminishment and both are hungry for love and life. How we act that out depends on personalities, circumstances, and choices that we make. As the hunger becomes more and more urgent, the vampire's soul shrivels and desiccates. The vampire stops seeing the victim as a valuable and worthwhile human and begins to see him or her as fodder. Often vampires bind their prey to them with ties of affection, need, guilt, or shame.

Vampires are often the ones who have every reason why a relationship should continue. They are masters at manipulation, disregarding boundaries (just this one time, of course) and paralyzing the prey. The problem is that vampires abdicate responsibility for supplying their own needs. Instead they feed on what others already have, giving nothing in return.

Often we learn to be predator, prey, or both from our society, our family, and our relationships. We see people around us praised for giving and giving without counting the cost, and others for being aggressive and taking all they can.

Vampires come in many styles. An obvious one is the strong "Dracula" type with the charisma and the enchanting personality. This vampire fascinates us with what seems to be great power and seduces us with the promise of being "special," of having a chance to partake in the vampire's power or protection. Often this vampire will show concern for the prey, but it is not a caring based in equality. You might care the same way for the food in your refrigerator.

We see this vampire in many relationships that include violence. The violence in the relationship generates emotional heat, something that is sustaining to the vampire. The greater this heat, the more satisfying the feeding. Somehow the predator gains strength from making the prey weaker and weaker, blaming the prey for any failing, real or imagined.

When the predator has gone too far—perhaps striking the prey—the air of mystery turns to gushing charm, profuse apologies, gifts to make it up, promises never to do it again. The truth is that the predator has learned that this cycle of violence can go on and the prey will not leave. Thus the vampire has ensured the source of emotional heat to continue to feed the insatiable hunger.

THE POWER OF "AND"

The vampire can be a charismatic leader or personality, one who takes pride in being strong enough to tackle strong prey. Steven, who had grown up feeling awkward because of his intelligence and good grades, was stunned when he met Sarah, who was his equal or better in brain power, and witty and charming too! They began to date, and they took pleasure in showing off their intelligence and accomplishments to each other.

Yet over time this began to feel uncomfortable. It almost seemed as if they were in some sort of contest to see who would win. Steven would come home from a date feeling as if he was always on his guard. "Losing" their "game" could be as simple as being ten minutes late. He felt that Sarah sucked all the juice out of him, almost gloating over his perceived failure.

He realized that breaking up with her might solve the immediate problem, but he wanted to dig a little deeper so that he would not find himself in the same situation again. He looked over his past romantic relationships and noticed there was a pattern. Either he selected someone who was "equal or better" or he chose someone who placed him on that same pedestal. As he considered this, he realized that his relationships had a consistent element of competition that resulted in one partner feeding on the mistakes of the other.

Steven had set this up by choosing to "grade" people and himself. In valuing Sarah for her "better-than" qualities, in showing her off to his friends, in seeing himself as the "winner" when he scored some small point off her, he had fed on her life force as she had on his. It took a while for Steven to see how clearly he had been both prey and vampire. It was much easier to see himself as the wronged party instead of recognizing how both had failed to understand each other as whole people.

What he eventually learned was that he did not need to compare himself with the people around him. He was who he was, and that was enough. He could enjoy and appreciate others, but that did not diminish him. He started this process by listing every day ten things that he liked about himself and that he was grateful for, without repeating. One day his list might include appreciating his ability to solve a problem at work, his achievement in bench-pressing ten more pounds, and his own thoughtfulness in remembering to call an old friend. Another day he might appreciate how good he looked in that blue shirt and the work he had done to clean up his home.

After just a short time, he had a long list of things he liked about himself and that he was grateful for. He would reread the list when he felt "less than" or "empty."

One of the hardest habits for Steven to break was comparing himself with others. What finally worked was a simple word: "and." If he saw that a colleague was being praised, if he met someone who challenged his self-confidence, if he somehow felt diminished by someone else, he trained himself to say "and." "Brenda did an excellent job AND I can choose to praise her also." "That woman over there is intelligent and fascinating AND I can praise my own good qualities." "Jerry is a great golfer AND there is plenty of praise to go around."

In this next story, Jane tells of losing her own hopes and

part of her spirituality to a relationship that could have used the power of "and."

————————————— *Jane Speaks* —————————————

Partners in a relationship can find themselves understanding and experiencing spiritual life in very different ways—even when they belong to the same religion. This is perhaps especially true in Pagan religions, with their emphasis on personal responsibility and the creative force of building new spiritual paths.

At one point, I was in a relationship with a Wiccan who brought me into his coven. He later decided to start a new Wiccan group, and he did not invite me to join. He said that in his meditations, his patron goddess had indicated I was not welcome.

I was hurt and disappointed. I felt excluded from his religious life, from the hopes that I had for a spiritually charged partnership. I don't believe my ex-partner intended to be a vampire; indeed, much later it turned out that he had experienced some of my actions as vampiric. Yet intentional or not, this spiritual separation became part of a larger set of resentments that led to our parting ways completely.

Though the experience was painful, it also taught me something about the nature of spiritual information. We may learn things from the Divine, but we filter them through our own hearts and minds. If we are out of balance, then we interpret that information in ways that are out of balance. I'm sure my ex-partner was truthful about his experience. But I'm also sure that a part of him was using this as a way to express his own unhappiness in our relationship.

Later, I prayed to this goddess myself, and found Her welcoming and inspiring. Through worshiping Her I found some of the healing I needed, and I began to reconnect to my religion as a source of abundance and renewal.

When my husband Cassius and I got together, it was clear that we had a lot in common spiritually. We'd both been trained as Wiccans, using similar systems. Yet there was a difference: His interests had led him to spend a great deal of time researching and worshiping the Roman gods, where my interest had primarily been in Celtic deities. It was important to both of us that our relationship have a shared spiritual component, but it was also important for us not to leave behind the work we'd done up to that point.

We could have solved this any number of ways, but fortunately, history provided an answer: Roman and Celtic people had spent centuries in the same areas, sharing religious information, so we could draw on historical ideas from both cultures as we built a shared spiritual practice. Learning about the Celto-Roman period together, and worshiping its gods together, helped us establish our balance. It allowed us each to draw on our own expertise and to learn from the other's work while building up new stores of information, both historical and intuitive.

THE GREAT VAMPIRE HUNT

We can figure out if we have been in the presence of a vampire by looking at three things.

We may feel drained or depleted, as Carrie did in the earlier example.

We notice that we need to be filled, but no matter how we try to fill the void, it is not enough. We go shopping or we eat the third candy bar or we sleep six extra hours or we scrub the house—but we are not satisfied. We are disconnected from our source of spiritual strength; we are out of balance.

Barry worked for a company that left him feeling this way. The money was good, and he was able to buy his first new car. After the newness wore off, though, he still felt empty. Over the next few years, he bought a boat, a motorcycle, and a different car. But he was still empty. For Barry, it might have been more helpful to use the old car to drive to a new job! He was failing to balance his commitments to his own sanity, health, and emotional well-being with the practical considerations of earning a living.

We find ourselves violating our own moral code. For most of us, our ethics come from the same place as our spiritual energy. When our actions and words don't back up our ethics, it's a pretty sure sign we've lost touch with ourselves and the Divine.

Casey found herself yelling at her children over silly stuff. She had been raised in a home where voices were often loud, and she had made a commitment to herself not to raise her voice unnecessarily in her home. At the same time, she noticed that her sister-in-law often called to talk about her physical problems. Casey's suggestions (such as going to the doctor) went nowhere as her sister-in-law continued to wallow in self-imposed misery. When Casey cut off the phone calls, she found she was able to give more of her patience to the children. Casey had been harming the kids while trying to avoid offending her sister-in-law.

All of these are ways of expressing anger—the signal that something is wrong.

Anger: Too Important to Ignore

Where do emotions come from? Most people will say "the heart" or "the mind" or even "other people's stupidity." While those answers may be partly right, the true source of anger is our own bodies. Emotions are the signals our bodies send us about our perceptions of the world and the people around us. Emotions are simply signals, not "right" or "wrong" in themselves.

Anger is nothing more and nothing less than a signal that something is wrong. We are responsible for what we choose to do with our anger. But first we have to identify the emotion—a difficult thing to do if we begin by saying "I never get angry."

Everyone gets angry. There are many things "wrong" in our lives—simple things such as having to get up early, and complicated things such as international terrorism. When we become angry, our bodies and minds generate energy. Identifying the type of anger we are experiencing can help us to choose productive ways of using that energy.

Think of anger as a traffic light. We have traffic lights at places where there are potential problems. The presence of the signal alerts us to potential danger and gives us a way to avoid harm. But we have to choose to identify the problem (cross traffic) and take appropriate action (obey the signal). To pretend the signal isn't there is to invite an accident.

We can separate anger into three kinds: green, yellow, and red. The type of anger is neither right nor wrong, just as the lights are not right nor wrong. Our own interpretations and actions give value to the ethically neutral light.

Green anger occurs when we know something is wrong, but we choose to proceed anyway. For example, you are in the fifth grade and are about to take a social-studies test. You spent the entire weekend studying chapter 7. You know so much about Mexico that you want to move south and trade in your German shepherd for a Chihuahua. Then you get to the test, and it's on chapter 8—not Mexico, but Japan. You are very angry—mostly with yourself—but you take the test anyway. You use your anger energy to do the best you can and to resolve to double-check the next assignment before you study.

Yellow anger occurs when we know something is wrong, but we choose to proceed cautiously. For example, the phone rings at 9:00 P.M. It's your boss's wife. You have not heard from her since last summer, when they needed volunteers to supervise her son's scout troop's overnight trip. Visions of fourteen unruly seventh- and eighth-graders packed into a camper dance in your head.

She begins the conversation with a cheery greeting and the fateful question: "What are you doing this weekend?" Immediately, you feel angry. You use your energy to stay focused on responding cautiously, keeping in mind your schedule and her relation to your boss. Your response might be a cautious "Why do you ask?"

Red anger occurs when we know something is wrong and we want it stopped now. For example, you've just bought a new jacket and are walking toward your car in the mall parking lot. Someone grabs your shopping bag bag and runs away. You use your energy to yell "Stop thief!" at the top of your lungs.

Some anger feels so big that it would destroy the world if it were allowed free rein. Some anger is so small that we ignore it for a while until it comes back to bite us. Some anger seems wrong, such as being mad at the gods or the dog or at someone who is sick. Some anger seems useless. No matter how "wrong" it seems, the first step is to identify it as anger.

One way or another, whether we acknowledge it or not, the energy of our anger will be used. We might turn that energy in on ourselves, which becomes depression. We use the energy creatively to bike or draw or clean or weed. Or sometimes we send the energy toward someone or something that isn't part of what generated it, such as yelling at the cat because we had a bad day at work. Learning to identify anger and work with it in a helpful way is not always easy, but it is worth the effort. If we respect our bodies' signals that something is wrong, we can begin to look for the area or areas where we are out of balance.

The following myth, which has grown from a controversial Jewish text of the early medieval period, is a symbolic way of describing what can happen to the energy of anger when it does not find a positive outlet.

Myth: The First Wife

The Old Testament tells us how God created Adam, the first male, from the earth. In the present story, we find that Eve was Adam's second wife. The first, it seems, was a lady named Lilith. The name comes from the ancient world, though this story only dates back to the eighth century or so.

It goes like this: Lilith was made by God from the earth, in the same way that Adam was. Because of this she considered herself Adam's equal, and she refused his demand that she always take the bottom position during their coupling. They argued, and Adam told her she had to lie beneath him because he was her superior. Seeing that this fight was getting her nowhere, Lilith left by pronouncing a magical name of God, which gave her the power to fly away.

Adam complained to his Maker, and God sent three angels to bring Lilith back. They found her far from Eden, making love to lascivious demons and bearing hundreds of demon-children ("lilim") every day.

The angels gave her the message from God: Either she went back to Adam, or a hundred of her demon-children would die every day. She refused to return, and the angels threatened to kill her. Still she refused. She had been given powers and would not give them up. Lilith was the demoness who caused newborn infants to die. She gave her angelic messengers one concession: She promised to spare any baby who wore an amulet with the angels' names on it.

Think of Lilith when you seem to be squashing anger instead of working through it. Unresolved anger and resentment breed like Lilith's demons. By allowing them to build up, we end up spending time and energy hurting ourselves and the ones we care for, giving "birth" to unhealthy, unproductive patterns that take the place of health, strength, creativity, and love.

The following case indicates there was plenty of anger to go around.

AN UNCONVENTIONAL ARRANGEMENT

Anthony, a business writer, and Gwen, a speech pathologist, were married and belonged to a coven where sexual expression was a part of the ritual structure. After years of living in apartments, in their early fifties they managed to buy a dilapidated old house. To fund their renovations, they rented a room to Penny, who worked with Anthony at a local business magazine.

About a month after they moved in, Gwen came home early from work and surprised Anthony and Penny who were making love on the couch! As Penny fled to her room, it was clear that Gwen was very angry, so angry that she stood seething, unable to put her emotions into words. Thrown off by her silence, Anthony stammered out rationalizations: "It was nothing really. We're all naked together in the hot tub, right? And we're Pagans! We're above all those boring old conventionalities, aren't we?"

Gwen didn't say a word. Anthony's excuses sounded more and more hollow, then ran out. Finally, he began to talk about what was really going on for him. Amid the pressure of moving and getting the home ready for the insurance inspector, their emotional and sensual life had become less of a priority, and he felt lonely. He and Gwen both considered themselves to be "children of the sixties" and had even discussed communal living. He also had long been drawn to the idea of a polyamorous relationship. He told Gwen he wanted to take Penny as a secondary partner.

Gwen was familiar with the idea of polyamory. They'd had a few friends who engaged in relationships of this kind. She wasn't necessarily opposed to the idea—but this was not the way to bring it up.

Gwen realized that she and Anthony had made a lot of assumptions about the fundamental basis of their relationship, and had never set boundaries or rules for themselves. Before tackling that issue, though, Gwen needed time to think. "I'm very angry, and it's going to be a while before I feel like talking to you again," she told him.

Gwen was sure the quiet, vulnerable Penny had not initiated sex with Anthony. She knocked on the door of Penny's room and asked to talk. Gwen was familiar with vampiric relationships and had no trouble recognizing what had happened to Penny. It saddened her to think of her husband as someone who would drain another's life force.

Penny was genuinely horrified at Gwen's anger, and she launched into a long apology. Gwen listened, then said carefully, "I'm too close to this situation to judge, Penny, and while I'm hurting right now, I don't think it was your fault. I do hope you can talk about this with someone who can help you process it."

She also made a request: "Anthony and I have a lot of talking to do, and it probably isn't going to be very peaceful around here. Is there someone you could stay with for a day or two?" Penny agreed and went to the phone to call a friend.

Leaving Penny's room, Gwen sighed and took stock. Her right hand was clenched in a fist, her jaw was taut, her body seemed charged with energy. She was still too angry to talk with Anthony again. She took a brisk walk to burn off some of the excess steam. The exercise quieted her body but not her mind. She pulled out a long-forgotten set of mosaic tiles and assembled six of them to serve in the Marbles exercise (see appendix).

Gwen drew two neutral tiles and one red one. The red anger was easy to identify: She wanted Anthony's behavior to stop, and this was not a feeling that was likely to go away. Yet it also seemed that now was not the time to act. She needed to gain a little distance before deciding what to do next.

Anthony knew he had made a mistake. Over the next couple of days, he realized just how big a mistake it was. What he couldn't figure out was what he was supposed to do next. Gwen was giving him freezing looks every time she saw him, and Penny had left for a couple of days, maybe longer. He thought he knew Gwen, and he appreciated her open mind and unconventional spirit—yet here she was acting so aloof. He had thought it would be great living in a house with two beautiful women, and here he was unable to get near either of them.

Frustrated, he pulled out his Tarot cards and did the Balance reading to get some advice.

Interpretation. Anthony has turned his back on the gifts and treasures of his own life and has allowed a desire for adventure and new things to play out in a way that impedes his personal progress. He and Gwen have done a good job of founding an equal partnership, but now it's time for that partnership to move into a new phase. The Chariot reversed in the Consensus position shows the ill effects of his decision to expand his sexual horizons without consulting Gwen. They are both at a stage of their lives where they have material prosperity and a degree of emotional knowledge. The reversed 5 of Swords shows Anthony's efforts to vindicate himself in Gwen's eyes. His action has violated a boundary and thrown their relationship off balance.

In choosing the foundation card for the second half of the reading, Anthony looked first at the reversed cards in his "compass." There were three of them, but only one Major Arcana card, so he chose that one, the Chariot.

The next part of the reading dealt with how to resolve the Consensus issues in the situation:

Interpretation.   Anthony must repair the damage he did when he acted outside of consensus in a matter that concerned both himself and Gwen. The practical advice is to refrain from pleasure seeking and recognize that a positive outcome will require work. Emotional poverty will result unless Anthony and Gwen can renew their faith in each other. Spiritually, Anthony is advised not to spurn the gifts he has, but to treat them with appreciation and joy. The outcome indicates hard work ahead for Anthony, but work that will earn him a just reward.

This information told Anthony he had to take on the hard work of reconciling with Gwen before moving to satisfy his urge for novelty and pleasure. He started by writing a full apology—not "I'm sorry you felt that way" or "I'm sorry but let me justify myself," but simply "What I did was wrong. I realize you are hurt and angry, and I regret what I did." He ended by declaring that he loved her, he wanted to stay in the marriage, and he was willing to work to earn back her trust. He left this letter on her bureau and left the house for a while to give her time to read and understand it.

It's difficult to sustain a white-hot fury over a long period,

and Gwen was already much calmer by the time she received the letter. It was not everything she needed from Anthony, but it was enough to get her to talk with him again. She still felt betrayed and rejected, but she also realized that tears and re-criminations weren't going to save their marriage.

She asked Anthony to think about what needs he was try-ing to fulfill in seeking a new sexual relationship, and he was able to speak clearly about the urges that had led him to ap-proach Penny. Gwen said that since they hadn't established rules for their relationship, she couldn't fully blame him for going outside their marriage. She was angry about that but more angry that he hadn't felt he could talk to her about it.

She asked him to work with her toward consensus and trust, starting with negotiating a new understanding of the structure of their marriage. To start, she suggested that while he would no doubt continue to interact with Penny at work, perhaps they should ask her to find another place to live.

Over the next couple of weeks, Gwen and Anthony estab-lished a set of rules they could both live with. They agreed to choose each other as primary partners but not to be sexually exclusive. They promised to consult each other before initiat-ing any outside sexual encounter, and they agreed to refrain if the other person could not freely give permission to proceed. On the practical side, Anthony and Gwen agreed that "dates" outside the marriage would not take precedent over their plans as a couple and would not take place on worknights.

To mark their fresh start, and to honor the spirituality that gave them strength, they did the Fivefold Blessing (see appen-dix) to honor each other as spiritual beings. They chose to do this "skyclad" (nude), as they had done many times before.

It was a bit uncomfortable to be naked together after all that had passed. This blessing and this trust were important to them in their spiritual practice, so they stayed with the feeling until they were ready to proceed. After the blessings, they re-mained in silence for a time, holding each other. They knew this wasn't a solution, but a beginning. There was still much work to be done to rebuild and reinforce their trust and communication. Now, at least, the work had begun.

During the next summer, they had a house guest—Chloe, who had been Gwen's roommate in college. Chloe had just gone through a divorce, and this was a time for her to relax with old friends and to make some decisions about what she wanted to do with her life. The divorce left Chloe without a job (she had worked in her ex-husband's business) or a house. She found that she had no deep emotional ties to the place where she had lived for her married life. With her children grown and living in other cities, she found herself able to make choices that just suited her.

The two-week visit became three weeks, then four. Chloe's wallpapering and drywall skills were very welcome as the three of them renovated the second floor. Anthony's expertise gleaned from his work as a business writer was just what Chloe needed to help her figure out what to do with her divorce settlement. Gwen and Chloe were able to draw on their long relationship and knowledge of each other's lives to grow even closer.

Gwen and Anthony realized how much they enjoyed having Chloe as a part of their lives. They discussed their agreement to be primary with each other and decided that while it had served them until now, the old dream of communal living might just be possible with Chloe. Together the couple decided to ask their friend to consider handfasting to them both for a year and a day. In that time, they would explore how they got along in a committed relationship, including how they might or might not interact sexually, and then decide whether to continue.

The three of them discussed this over the next weeks and decided that they wanted to try it. Anthony explained how helpful the Balance Tarot Spread had been to him when they were in crisis, and Chloe was interested to see what the cards

had to say about the three of them. Instead of a single foundation card, all three put their energy into the deck and each
pulled a card to represent what they brought to the relationship
as a foundation.

Interpretation.   Chloe's signifier indicates a giving person
whose gifts are valued. Anthony's card shows a man who had
fought many battles alone, but who is now interested in a coop-
erative rather than a competitive way of living. Gwen's reversed
8 of Pentacles indicates she has done good work, but it is now
time to become independent and take control of her own life,
regardless of what more traditional teachers have said. She saw
this as permission to experiment with new ways to be in relationship. The High Priestess in their current situation shows
the strong spiritual potential of their plan.

Each of them has experienced difficult journeys in trying
to bring equality to their lives, and it is important for them to
recognize and respect one another's time, energy, and resources. There is a potential for power struggles, and the commitment to work together may not be easy. They each bring
emotional baggage to this moment, and there will be emotional
consequences for the choices they make. As a partnership they
are likely to be secure financially and able to manage practical
matters, provided that they recognize this as a new beginning
and are willing to set aside old habits and resentments. They
each need to be aware that their way is not the only way, or the
only right way.

They returned all but the Ace of Wands to the deck, and
began the second part of the reading. The practical advice reaffirmed what the first part had said:

The practical advice is to be aware of potential conflicts
and make fair and reasonable choices. The emotional advice
points out that they aren't children, that they all bring a great
deal of experience to the relationship. This has both positive
and negative connotations: They may be "set in their ways" and

TOP

find it hard to adjust, but they also may have learned over time not to sweat the small stuff. In any case, they need to be very careful not to make "sunny" assumptions just because things feel good now. The spiritual advice emphasizes the need to work in equality and consensus rather than letting one party take charge. The outcome, assuming they followed the advice and cautions, was great personal fulfillment and prosperity.

The reading made it clear that they needed to be extra careful not to let things go unsaid. Gwen knew Chloe was still working on expressing uncomfortable emotions. She shared the Marbles exercise with her friend, emphasizing that anger is only a signal that something is wrong and encouraging Chloe to use the exercise to sort out her own emotional state. She asked Chloe to pull three tiles to see if anything else needed to be said. Chloe said she was nervous about pulling the tiles because she had felt so positive about the reading. What if there *was* some underlying emotional problem?

The first tile was neutral. Chloe said this reflected her comfort with the caring she sensed from Gwen and Anthony.

The second tile was also neutral. Chloe saw this as an affirmation of having dealt with some of her fears about her financial future, thanks to Anthony's help.

And the third tile was—neutral! There were no hidden problems. Reassured, Chloe began to look around her and realize, "This is home."

─────────────── *Cynthia Speaks* ───────────────

When Chris and I first chose to live together, to be handfast and eventually to marry, we chose the balance of our relationship by agreeing to a shared vision of relationship that we called ''primary.''

We honored the Spirit, the Center, by choosing each other as primary—the most important, first, essential relationship after our relationship with ourselves and with the Divine.

This vow between us did not include sexual fidelity. We were both free, within the bounds of physical safety and no possibility of pregnancy, to be sensual or sexual with whomever we chose. We trusted each other's judgment and did not have to ask permission nor exercise a veto.

However, we were very clear with our outside partners. Anyone else either of us was intimate with knew beforehand that there were no secrets between Chris and me, and that we took priority in each other's hearts. Because Chris and I were primary with each other, even regular, long-standing loves outside the relationship were "always new." This meant that each encounter with another was not assumed but negotiated on a single-time basis. We did not make assumptions about our lovers.

Another important aspect was that we chose to act from abundance, not from need. We went outside our relationship only if things were good between us. If either or both of us had a problem between us, we solved that first. We had no desire to use another person nor to betray our commitment to each other.

During his illness, there was not a time I can recall when the primacy of Chris in my heart wavered. I had no desire to be sexually intimate with anyone else. Chris urged me to take a lover, because his illness meant sexuality between us was virtually nonexistent. The other aspects of our relationship were more than enough for me at the time. I was fortunate that our relationship was strong enough to see me through his death—and beyond, for I still communicate with him in meditation and welcome his unseen presence at rituals and important events.

I believe that because Chris and I practiced the Principles, when he finally died, I was able to grieve for him without regrets. The grief felt clean, uncomplicated, though it shook my very soul and at times still does.

When he died, I chose to be primary with myself for a time, to allow myself to heal, to grieve, and to recenter myself. As the abundance of my own self and my relationship with the Divine was renewed, and because that relationship was good and satisfying, I found I was ready to be social again. In fantasy, I could not imagine another man who would be as wonderful and precious to me as Chris had been. I figured that my next serious relationship would be with a woman. I was wrong.

I was attending a national convention in my hometown. In meditation on Thursday morning, Chris "told" me he had a surprise for me and wouldn't tell me what. I met many new people at the event, but when I greeted a particular one, I heard Chris say in my mind, "Surprise!"

So over the next few days, Harry and I talked. And it turned out that he not only approved of the Principles, but he had been working with something similar in his own life. And he was Pagan. And adorable. And available. And interested.

In less than a month, he had quit his job and moved five hundred miles to be with me. We've been together ever since, still practicing the Principles and very much in love. One addition to the "rules" for Harry and me is that whenever possible, we sleep together and wake up in the same bed.

The way Chris and I did, and now Harry and I do, structure our relationship is only one of many. I have not seen a relationship of any kind, no matter what its sexual codes, that works well and satisfactorily over time if the first four Principles are consistently violated.

Abundance, Not Need

On her weekend retreat, Vicki went through a great deal of powerful thinking and talking about the sexual abuse she had suffered as a child and the ways it had affected her adult life. Meanwhile, George had found forty-eight hours of solo parenting more challenging than he'd expected. He was exhausted from mopping up spills, arguing over meals and bedtimes, dealing with little Tim's stomach upset, and trying to keep the house somewhat clean for Vicki's return. George was so delighted to see her that he forgot his resolve to give her space physically and went running up with the children to greet her with a big hug. Deep in thought, she sidestepped his embrace, greeted the children absentmindedly, and went straight to her living room chair to go over her notes from the sessions.

"Well, *that* was heartwarming," he couldn't help muttering under his breath. Then he marshaled his tired thoughts and spent a moment thinking about what he could freely give at that moment, and what he wanted to receive. "Excuse me," he said to Vicki, trying to keep the resentment out of his voice. "I see you have a lot on your mind, but I'm very tired and I'd like to ask if you could help me by giving the kids their baths."

Vicki looked at him for the first time and saw how drained he really was. "Okay, I'll do bath time. We'll talk when you're feeling less tired."

Later, when the children were in bed and George had had a chance to grab a few minutes of peace, Vicki said, "I know you were angry with me earlier, and I'm sorry I didn't seem to respond to you. I've got so much to think about, and I really need some time to process it all before I try to apply it to life here."

"Oh, it's okay," sighed George. He really was still angry but was trying to get past it. "Thanks for your help."

"Are you awake enough to hear some of the things I thought about this weekend? Or should we wait till tomorrow?"

He thought for a minute. "Go ahead."

"Okay, I'll just talk about one thing. One of the workshops we did was about choosing a personal symbol and meditating on it. So I decided to choose a random card out of my Tarot deck. It came up the Star card." She took it from her deck and put it on the table. The image—a beautiful, nude woman pouring water into a pool, with stars around her head—was one George had seen many times before. At that moment, the woman on the card almost seemed like a taunt to his sexual urges, and he struggled to set aside his resentment and hear what Vicki was saying.

"We meditated on our cards and spent a lot of time talking about what each of us saw during the meditation and what it meant for us. For me, the message of this card was wonderful and strong, so strong it almost scared me! What came to me in this meditation was the sense of *abundance*—the sense that there *is* enough of whatever I want in the world, that I *am* enough to be whatever I need to be. I'm good enough, strong enough, pretty enough, smart enough. I didn't get to experience those feelings as a child. I finally feel complete and whole. And I know this may not have the same resonance for you, because you couldn't share my experience, but I wanted to tell you, because it was a really important insight for me."

From this, she told him, she had gained strength around her own sexuality. No, she wasn't going to suddenly become passionate in bed, but she would no longer defend her own body like a fortress under siege. By perceiving her love and sexuality as coming from this place of abundance, she was able to freely choose to be "primary" with herself, perceiving herself as a strong decision maker, a Star rather than a victim.

George understood that she still didn't want to make love, but he was too tired to take in much more. He did understand that Vicki had come to some kind of powerful insight, and he found his anger had dissipated and he was ready to be happy for her. "I'm glad that happened for you," he said. "I really need to go to sleep now."

Over the next few days, George thought about the idea of being primary with oneself and about his earlier work in which he realized that Vicki was not responsible for making him happy. He asked her to explain the notion of "primary with oneself" again and, after thinking about it, resolved to choose himself as his first focus of respect and care rather than using himself as a second-best lover.

George also realized he needed better ways to deal with anger. He saw that his resentment was draining his own energy—almost as if he were in a vampiric relationship with himself—and keeping him from fully hearing and understanding Vicki. In doing some research on anger, he came across the notion of "green," "yellow," and "red" anger, and he decided to do the Marbles exercise.

George drew two yellow marbles and a neutral one. The message of this was caution in two ways. First, he needed to be cautious, because whatever he was angry at might not really be the problem. Second, he needed to act with caution in dealing with that object of anger, to be aware that he was not seeing the whole picture.

He applied this to his most recent experience of anger, when he'd been upset that Vicki didn't greet him or reassume her role in the household immediately on her return. George was able to congratulate himself for not blowing up at her, and for asking for what he needed.

He also realized that in that moment he hadn't been aware of the positive steps she'd taken toward recovering her ability to be confident and loving. Venting his anger then, he saw, might have encouraged her to shut down, to move away from him. Even in his exhaustion that night, he realized, he'd learned enough to give her room to move toward him, and he was able to feel proud of himself.

For Vicki, the Balance reading was a welcome confirmation that she had indeed made progress, both as a person and as a partner.

Interpretation.   Vicki's current situation stems from a "nightmare"—the terror of her abuse revisited. She has turned this horrible awakening to positive purposes by learning new skills and by working to become a better person. The 7 of Cups in the East indicates she and George have done a good job in establishing equality, in at least envisioning a healthy, happy relationship. The Page of Wands in the South shows them both as energetic in their work of learning to share power and move toward the next phase of their marriage. The 4 of Cups is the only reversed card, depicting Vicki as rejecting the emotional gifts that come her way, from both her partner and herself. The

Justice card shows her and George as wise and fair in their giving and receiving. In the center, Vicki is the Emperor, seizing control of her own spirituality and learning to perceive herself as powerful rather than powerless.

Since there was only one reversed card, Vicki moved the 4 of Cups to the second half of the reading:

Interpretation. In the practical realm, Vicki can better learn to understand and enjoy the good things in her life when she stops trying to be the "earth mother" Empress, stops trying to be everything to everyone, giving energy she doesn't have. This will mean some changes in her day-to-day world as she rebalances her activities to focus on what's most important. Emotionally, the reversed Knight of Swords tells her not to rush off to find or become something new. Spiritually, the 9 of Pentacles reminds Vicki that she has already been given everything she needs. The reversed Hierophant tells her the solution lies in refusing to accept power struggles. Instead of trying to win battles with George, she will do well to balance herself emotionally and seek new ways to look at problems.

This reading gave Vicki a great deal of food for thought. She was able to see her own progress and to congratulate herself on the learning and growth that had come out of her crisis. She also saw that this time of trouble would ultimately make for a stronger, happier marriage, and for this she was grateful. Finally she understood that in marriage, win-lose situations— George wants sex, I don't give it to him—ultimately gave no joy to either party.

George and Vicki realized that unexpressed anger, and their fear of each other's anger, were still obstacles in their relationship. In the Three Buttons ritual (found in the *Spellbook* in appendix), they empowered a set of symbols to help them communicate anger without confrontation.

The Three Buttons are personal symbols that partners can

use to express anger without confrontation. If George was angry at Vicki, he would place one, two, or three buttons—depending on the strength and urgency of his anger—on her bureau. She did the same for him.

Using the buttons gave them time to think and space to respond without having to deal with a blast of resentment. They found that after a while, they could often figure out what one button was about and work to make things better before the situation became a two-button problem.

They used the buttons to start new negotiations of household duties and child care. This meant some adjustments as George realized it was up to him to take responsibility for 50 percent of the work, and Vicki gave up her role of being responsible for all of it.

One Tuesday, George got home from the office, went to change out of his necktie, and found a button on his bureau. He couldn't remember anything he'd done that might have irritated Vicki. Puzzled, he took it to the kitchen, where Vicki was feeding the children. He held it up and gave her a questioning look. "Later," she said, and he began preparing the adults' meal. All through bath time, bedtime stories, and cleaning up the kitchen, he wondered what on earth she could want.

Finally, with the last load of laundry in and the house settling down for the evening, George found Vicki in the living room. "What's with this?" he asked, holding out the button. "Did I forget something?" She smiled. "Well, there *is* something wrong between us. You haven't given me a hug in a long time, and I want one." George was taken aback for a moment; then he sat next to her and put his arm around her. She didn't turn away or stiffen. In fact, she sat up and pulled him into a warm, tender kiss.

"You know, we've both been through a lot lately," she said. "Maybe it's time we tried another weekend away—you know, just the two of us."

The Gift of Balance

In many ways, the Principles are more like a circle or spiral than a line. If your relationship doesn't reflect the Principle of Balance, if something feels harmful to your spirit, if you feel angry, it may be that you need to go back to the beginning, to start with Equals.

Acknowledging and honoring your spiritual self is, as we've seen, essential to avoiding vampiric relationships, and they help you to become the best partner you can be. The form of your spirituality is not as important as simply knowing you have it and can draw on it to help you solve problems in your life.

Pagan religions acknowledge the possibility of multiple ways to structure a relationship. This freedom carries with it a responsibility to understand the consequences of each choice you make. Whatever form you decide on, you may find it worthwhile to reexamine your shared lives from time to time, looking for signs of imbalance and working on small problems before they become large ones. Many situations can be resolved, or at least brought closer to resolution, by applying the Principles of this book.

In particular, keep the Principle of Balance with you. When you find yourself burying your feelings or avoiding conversations that go below the surface, look at your life to see what's out of balance. Is it physical? Emotional? Intellectual? Spiritual? If you are angry, find a way to acknowledge it instead of burying it, using the energy as fuel rather than letting it drag you down.

To end this book, we'll offer some final words on the Principles and some resources for exploring some of the ideas we've introduced.

Conclusion

The Wheel of Love

The circle is completed, with Balance at the center. We hope you have learned something of value here. We hope you are able to apply that learning to make your own life better.

We cannot promise that things will be perfect for you. We cannot even say that they will be pretty good. Many healthy relationships have days in which partners wish they were single.

We *can* say that when you find yourself unhappy in your relationship, you may find information here that will help you to understand that feeling and take productive actions. Begin with Equals and consider the issue with respect to all the Principles.

People and circumstances change over time. This is natural and normal. Working on one issue may cause others to surface. This, too, is natural and normal. The Principles are a path tha may be walked many times within a relationship. When you've reached a resolution, it may feel wonderful. Enjoy that feeling, but know also that it's unrealistic to assume everything is "fixed" once and for all. The next time you need the Principles, they will be there. Revisit them with the intention of learning something new each time, and take pride in your willingness to consciously consider your relationships instead of just letting them happen.

We, Jane and Cynthia, are not perfect people, and our relationships are not perfect. The Principles have meaning for us, and we refer to them as we work on making our partnerships better and stronger.

When we began this book, we wanted our work to be useful, honorable, and beautiful. We wanted to give our readers real ways to help themselves and their partners. We wanted to do this with great attention to ethics, and we wanted to use skill and care in expressing our ideas. We invoked three deities to help us: Baubo, Brigantia, and Thoth.

Baubo

Cynthia Speaks

I have been a devotee of Baubo for many years. She is the crone goddess of the belly, of laughter, of female jokes, of obscenity. She is the woman who does a lewd dance and tells dirty jokes to Demeter, who is mourning for her lost Persephone. She brings earthiness, joy, and new perspective to a grim and stagnant situation. Through Baubo's influence, Demeter is herself renewed and able to grow fruitful again.

Baubo's archetype is reflected in the "old nurse" in many stories. ˑnderstands how precious the freshness of innocence is. She sees ˑhe defensive walls people erect around themselves. She often ˑ to safely lower the walls, and to reclaim the present

I asked for her blessing and energy that the book embody some of her spirit.

Brigantia

Jane Speaks

B rigantia is the patron deity of the coven my husband and I formed together. In history she was a goddess who watched over her tribe in northern England, leading them to success and inspiring their reputation for fierce defense of their lands. Her name may also be related to Brigid, the goddess of smithcraft, healing, and poetry. The Romans linked Brigantia with their Minerva, goddess of war, craftsmanship, and medicine.

Through Brigantia we forge well-crafted links with others and hone our own spirit. Through her we heal the wounds, new and old, that keep us from bringing our best energy to the goals we value most. Through her we defend what is most important to us. Through her we draw on the well of creativity, granting us fresh perspectives and an overarching sense of the beautiful.

I asked for her energy to bring this project to a successful completion. I give thanks for her protection for my husband and our marriage. In honoring Brigantia, I bring the source of my spiritual energy to this book.

Thoth

Cynthia and Jane Speak

H ealing, strength, laughter, and perspective—all wonderful qualities, but a book needs one thing more. We invoked Thoth, the Egyptian god of writing, to give our words power and meaning. To the

Egyptians, writing was a magical act, done in the service of the gods. We asked the same for our writing.

Besides inventing writing and numbers, Thoth was also the god of time and measure. We asked his aid in managing our time as we wrote, and making sure each idea got enough consideration—not too much or too little, but enough.

Finally, Thoth was the scribe who wrote down the value of each soul as it was weighed after death. To him we prayed that this book might be ethical, that it might be a force (however small) for healing and good in the world.

Why did we do all this? Because we believe in the gods and goddesses of our faith, and we call on them to help with the important things in our lives and our communities.

We believe good relationships are important. They start with knowing yourself, working to become a better person, and appreciating who you are right now. As you grow more confident and happy, you may change the ways you relate to partners. Those changes are part of your growth, and understanding them is part of understanding you.

We believe stable relationships—whatever form they may take—make our world better. Partners in a healthy relationship support each other through bad times and share their stability with their families and communities. The skills of maintaining a relationship are important in many areas of life—business, politics, families, art, and charitable work. As we develop these skills we grow more effective in all these parts of our world, becoming more productive and creative members of our society. We believe Pagan religions offer valuable tools and inspiration for building such partnerships.

We don't believe life will be sunshine and lollipops all the time. That would be boring! We believe in the challenge of knowing another person, in the value of making room in your heart and your life to share, and in the power of being truly yourself and sharing that self. We believe that real love—not obsession or infatuation or unhealthy dependence—takes many forms and that each one is important and right.

This book is about a process that leads to growth and healing. Each exercise, story, spell, or divination is only a small part of that flow. The adventures, the trials, and the difficult spots make it possible for us to stop and consider our path. Then we are free to choose what is truly best, and in deepest accord with the Divine.

We wish you learning and growth and those moments of joy that sustain and deepen a relationship. We wish you the love that is right for you and the courage to tackle the difficult tasks. We wish you peace and healing when you need them.

The journey, say the wise, is the reward. May your journey bring you wisdom, strength, and peace.

Appendix

The Relationship Spellbook

Most of these exercises and rituals are mentioned elsewhere in this book. They are presented here, apart from any narrative, so that the reader can apply them personally.

Basic Grounding Meditation

Do this meditation three times, slowly, with several moments of silence at every pause:

> Visualize a pillar of white light-energy rising slowly from the earth itself, flowing upward through your feet, to your knees, up to your hips, glowing through your belly, to your breast, along your arms, into your shoulders, through your neck, and up through your head. Feel each body part relax as it accepts the light-energy. Then, breathing deeply, feel the

light subside gently and slowly back into the earth, taking with it any tension, frustration, or emotion that could block you from being fully present with your feelings in this place.

Clarifying Questions

One of the hard parts about being in a relationship is knowing yourself. These questions may not all apply to your situation, but they are very helpful to focus attention on what is happening under the surface. They work best when you answer them off the top of your head, out loud, without stopping to think too hard. This keeps your internal editor at bay: The answers that will best help you are the ones that represent your true feelings, not the ones you think you *should* say.

Describe the situation in words: Who is involved? What is happening? Where is this happening? When does this happen? How does this happen? Why does this happen?

What do I want?   If I could wave my magic wand, what would happen? What would I do? What would others do? How would the situation change?

What is the very best thing that could possibly happen here?

What do I think?   What is my opinion? Who is right? Who is wrong?

What do I think is likely in this situation?   What has happened like this in the past?

What do I feel? What are my emotions?

(Be careful with thinking as opposed to feeling: Any time you can replace "feel" with "think" it is not a feeling. For example, "I feel you are wrong" can be expressed as "I think you are wrong," so it is a thinking, not a feeling. "I feel angry" cannot be expressed as "I think angry," so it is a feeling. By all means express the things you think about your situation, but make sure you also explore the feelings.)

What do I need?   What are the absolute, bottom-line basics in the situation? What is it I MUST have to continue my existence? What is the very least I must have and am willing to do all I can to get?

What is the worst thing that could happen? How would it affect me? Who would be involved? What would be happening? Where would it be happening? When would it be happening? How would it happen? Why would it happen?

What are the things I have control over? Can I change who does this and what they do or what happens? Can I change when this happens? Can I change where this happens? Can I change why this happens? Can I change how this happens?

What are the things I don't have control over?

What reality has to shift for my intention to be manifest? How can I bring that about through correspondences?

Equals Tarot Spread

Whether or not you believe Tarot readings are divinely inspired, the images and words often combine to help the reader or questioner gain a clearer understanding of a situation. Those who use Tarot cards regularly will often tell you that the cards' true worth is in helping you to better understand the present and the past, rather than in predicting the future.

To use this spread, work with a deck that makes sense to you, one that is free of energy associated with old problems or people. Do this when you are calm and receptive to what the cards suggest. Unless you've memorized the card meanings, read the meaning from the guidebook or a reference book, and note things that seem relevant, whether they are pleasant or not.

It is sometimes difficult to read for ourselves because we are too close to the situation. If this seems to be the case for you, ask a friend to help.

As you shuffle the cards, concentrate on these questions:

What forces are at work affecting the equality in our relation-ship? What should I work on first to achieve greater equality?

Lay out the cards as shown in the diagram. The numbers represent the order of the cards.

First, look at the card for the Self (Card 1). Then find any matches by number and suit. (If you're using a deck that has a different organizing principle than the seventy-eight cards of the Rider-Waite, you may need to consult its guidebook or be creative in drawing your own correspondences among different cards.)

Look at your Self card; then find any other cards that match the Self card's number or suit. Read those cards first. Next, find matches for the True Situation card and read those. Other cards are considered less important to the reading.

Blessings on Our Home

You can use this spell with a partner or alone. (It is considerate to ask permission from those who share your home before in-voking any particular energies in it.) Because this spell is affil-iated with the East, the direction of air, it uses incense to change the energy of the air around you. If you or anyone in the house dislikes incense, you can achieve the same result with a bell, changing the air by sound rather than by aroma.

Set up an altar as close as possible to the "center" of the home—either the physical or spiritual center. If you have a fireplace or hearth, use that. Prepare House Blessing Incense and place a blue or white candle on the altar. As you see fit, decorate the altar with personal items or natural things that seem to you to symbolize a happy home. On or near the altar, place the household object you seek to empower with your wishes for your home. If more than one person is participating, there should be an object for each person.

House Blessing Incense.   Blend equal parts of basil, dill, and St. John's wort (for protection and good fortune). Add

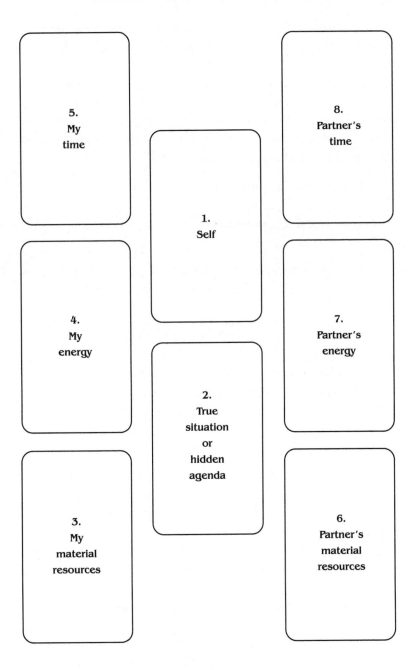

equal parts of lavender, rose petals, and rosemary (for partnership and bonding). Add a final part of frankincense (for purification).

Go to the easternmost point of your home and light charcoal for incense. If you have a partner with you, have one person hold the bowl and the other fan it with a feather. Proceed clockwise around the perimeter of the home, stopping at each window, door, and faucet to chant

> All that blocks our path, begone!
> Let this place be purified
> Let the cleansing now be done
> So say we who here reside!

After completing the circuit, go to your altar and light the candle. Invoke Vesta, goddess of the hearth (symbolized by the flame).

> Vesta, Keeper of Hearth, whose flame protects and purifies
>   the home,
> Warm this place with your love and harmony.
> Warm its people with your peace and understanding.
> Help me to act in concord with your energy, that I may learn
>   and grow.
> This I pray, O Vesta.

Speak in your own words to the goddess, and state the things you intend to do to make your home and your relationships more meaningful and harmonious. Solemnly promise that you will do these things, creating a definite statement for each action, and ask for divine help in sticking to your goals. ("Vesta, help me to pay more attention to the energy I bring home at the end of the workday.") If you are working with a partner, you might take turns making promises.

Next, touch or hold your symbolic object and state the qualities and energies that you wish to be a part of your home. Again, you can take turns if more than one person is doing this spell. Make these statements as definite as you can, both with your voice and your words, for by doing this you are invoking the energies you seek. ("May this home be filled with generosity! May this home be filled with welcoming light!") Do this for several minutes. It's okay to repeat things.

When you are done, thank the goddess and bid Her farewell. Let the candle burn as long as it is safe to do so. You may find it useful to burn a candle to Vesta at regular intervals as a reminder of your intent to create a harmonious home.

Talisman to Become a Better Partner

Many gods and goddesses are associated with wisdom, and any of them may be substituted here to match your own path. You may wish to decorate your space with some symbol of wisdom—perhaps sage incense, or a pearl necklace, or some apple-scented oil. Choose also an object that you will empower with the blessings of the goddess or god, something small but noticeable. You'll need some time and space in which you are not overtired or stressed and will not be disturbed. Set out a cup of juice or wine on your altar, and a little food to help you in grounding afterward.

Spend a few minutes in stillness, grounding and centering yourself. When you are ready, use a tool or your hands to inscribe a circle around your meditation area, using your own customary words or these:

> Circle of Power, I do conjure, stir and call thee. Let this
> be a place of wisdom, understanding, and light. So shall it
> be!

Face the East, looking at your symbol of divinity, and burn some sage incense or otherwise acknowledge a symbol of wisdom. Offer this invocation to Athena, or speak to your own deity in your own words:

Gray-eyed goddess of wisdom
Powerful protector and advisor
I ask your presence and your insight
I offer you my devotion willingly,
and willingly I accept your guidance.
Athena! Athena! Athena!

Assume a posture of meditation—sitting, standing, or lying down, whatever works for you—and wait until you feel that the goddess or god is ready to hear your prayer. (If you wait a few minutes and don't get this feeling, refocus on your intent, summon up your most sincere desire for the deity's aid, and repeat the invocation.)

Speak your prayer out loud or silently, but put it into words. Be honest—this is between you and the Divine One. Describe the problem and what you seek for yourself.

Most Pagans prohibit the manipulation of others through spellwork without their permission. This is simple courtesy and common sense. After all, you wouldn't want someone else manipulating you. When dealing with strong feelings and people to whom we're very close, it's especially important to be ethical. So make sure you're asking for qualities, feelings, and advice for yourself, not asking for other people to do what you want them to do.

Once you've described the problem and the goal you seek, close your eyes and create a mental image of yourself succeeding. See yourself as a strong, wise person with the power to solve problems, survive bad times, and enjoy good times as a helpful and positive partner. Spend some time on this, fixing the image firmly in your consciousness.

Holding this visualization at the back of your mind, open your eyes and take up the object you wish to empower, in both hands if possible. Describe yourself as if you were already that successful, glowing being you visualized, perhaps beginning something like this: "I am wise. I am filled with patience and understanding. I listen to my partner. I vent my frustrations and anxieties in ways that do not harm my family." Go on for as long as you can, with all the sincere intent you can muster to actually *be* this person. As you do this, you are infusing the item in your hands with the energy of this visualization.

When you are done, place the object back on the altar. Drink a toast to the Goddess or God:

Athena, Goddess of Wisdom, you have heard my prayers and
　my intentions.
I ask your aid in making them real.
I will make mistakes.
Forgive me for them, and help me to forgive myself.
I will accomplish my goals.
Accept my thanks, and help me to recognize my own suc-
　cesses.
I thank you, O Ancient One. Hail and farewell.

Close the circle and take time to ground yourself again before returning to the world. If you can do so, offer the rest of your cup's contents in a place of nature.

Place the object you have "charged" in a prominent location to remind you of the work you have done and the divine help you have sought. Choose a place where your object can be visible to you every day, especially in the situations that are most likely to become difficult or stressful.

Consensus Questions

Like the parties in a business negotiation, partners in a relationship need to think through their priorities and circumstances. This set of questions can help you to clarify your own ideas about an issue on which you and a partner need to achieve consensus. As with the Clarifying Questions, answer them aloud, off the top of your head, to get closer to what's really on your mind, not what you think you should say.

What do I really want? What is most important?

What right or rights do I want to exercise? What responsibilities go with them?

What kinds of pressure am I feeling? From whom?

What does my partner seem to want?

What is my bottom line? Is this worth my while?

What kind of time is involved here? Energy? Resources?

What hasn't worked so far?

What have I tried? What were the results?

Have other people been in a similar situation? What did they try? Did it work?

What approximates what I want? What conditions are present?

What are some options? List at least three that are not mentioned above, including playful ones.

One-Card Meditation

Consensus building has a lot to do with communicating—knowing and talking about your own thoughts and feelings, and hearing and accepting those of your partner. These thoughts and feelings include ideas that haven't been put into words yet, or intuitions that are set deep into your being. Tools such as Tarot help us to get in touch with these parts of ourselves by using imagery and symbolism.

This exercise uses a Tarot card as the catalyst for an active meditative experience. Its purpose, as in most divinations, is to help you get past your logical, rational mind and to get in touch with other senses. As you did in the Equals spread, you will begin by grounding, centering, and invoking whatever helpful powers you wish.

Hold the deck in your projective hand to invest it with your energy. Meditate briefly on the consensus issue, visualizing everyone being satisfied with the outcome. Then select a card with your "receiving" hand.

Look at the image, noticing as much as you can about it. Allow yourself to be drawn intuitively to some portion of the card. Close your eyes and imagine yourself in the picture, as any figure or object. Allow yourself to experience this, including any interactions that occur. Notice everything you can, including any changes that occur as you go into the card. Then open your eyes and consider the card again.

Repeat two more times, for a total of three different aspects of the same image. Thank those who helped you, ground the energy and write down your thoughts.

After you have done this, consider the insights and feeling that you may have had. Ask yourself:

What does this reflect about the situation?

What does this reflect about me?

What does this reflect about my partner?

What are some options suggested here that I may want to consider?

Brigid Prosperity Spell

The goal of this spell is to bring various kinds of abundance into our lives. It should not be done until you have taken some real-world steps toward achieving your goals. It calls on the Irish goddess Brigid, who governs smithcraft (our physical world and our work), healing (recovering from emotional as well as physical wounds), and poetry (our creative lives).

Each participant should gather a few small stones—one for each person doing the ritual, plus one more. These can be gathered in a place of nature, or can be quartz, agate, or other stones associated with your goals. Each stone should have at least one fairly smooth surface.

If you live near the ocean, obtain a container of seawater. Otherwise, dissolve some sea salt in a container of fresh water and leave it outside overnight. You'll need at least one permanent marker, a candle, and a cup or chalice with some drink all participants enjoy (wine, milk, or fruit juice are particularly suited to this). Set up a time and place where you can be undisturbed, and use music, lighting, and scent to help induce an atmosphere that is calming and centering.

In creating sacred space, you may choose to honor the Celtic realms (land, sea, and sky). Touch your hand or a wand or staff to the ground, saying:

Fruitful Land, support and uphold us.

Next, inscribe an outer boundary in the air with your hands or a tool.

Powerful sea, surround and protect us.

Finally, reach up toward the sky and say:

Radiant sky, guide and inspire us.

Remain together in meditation for a moment, then light the candle and invoke Brigid. This can be spoken by both together, by one partner alone, or by alternating lines:

Brigid, Queen of Poets
Brigid, Goddess of Healing
Brigid, Noble Lady of Smithcraft
We ask your presence at this rite
That our lives may be filled with abundance,
With craftsmanship and health,
With creativity and inspiration.
Hail to you, Bright Goddess of the Flame!

Dip each stone in the salt water, saying "I cleanse this stone of all impurities and the energies of others. Let the magic of this stone be given to our goals."

Using the marker, draw a symbol on each stone to represent a kind of abundance. The first is your own goal. The second is a goal you share as partners. The third and subsequent stones are a goal for each partner, a way of magically and spiritually expressing your support. This last one is tricky—it should be a goal the partner truly desires, not something *you* would like to see him or her achieve.

Talk about your symbols with one another as you draw, and check in to see if your choices of goals for your partner and the relationship are valid. The artwork doesn't have to be perfect—it just has to be meaningful to you. Abundance can take many forms—affection, wealth, friendship, growth of a garden, even pregnancy—so it's important to be specific.

When you are finished, set the stones aside to dry, then stand before your candle and hold the chalice together, saying:

Brigid of the Three Faces,
We ask your guidance and wisdom in creating prosperity.
We ask your healing and strength in manifesting abundance.
We ask your love and skill in using our riches wisely.
Fill this cup with your essence, that we may learn and grow
    in your ways.

Remain there for a moment, holding the chalice. Then one partner takes it and offers it to the other with these words: "Perfect love and perfect trust." This is a widely used Wiccan formula describing the trust that participants express in coming together for a ritual. In this case, it is also an affirmation of the goals of a relationship. We all know that no one can be perfect, but in this formula we offer our intention to love and trust to the greatest extent of our abilities.

The partner who has been offered the cup takes it and drinks, then offers it back with the same words. If more than two people are present, repeat this sequence so that each person offers and receives the cup with each other person. The remaining liquid may be poured on the ground after the ritual.

Each partner then picks up one stone at a time and speaks aloud its purpose, adding prayers, aloud or silently.

To energize the stones, place them between you, then stand or kneel facing one another. Rub your hands together until you feel a slight tingle in the palms, then reach out in front of you with both hands until your fingertips are just touching another person's, forming a circle and a circuit. As you remain in this position, just barely in contact, breathe deeply and let energy flow into the space between you, with the stones acting rather like batteries being charged. Stay here in silence for a few minutes, until you feel the stones are empowered with your combined intentions and essences.

When you are done, offer your thanks and farewells to Brigid, then bid "hail and farewell" to the sky, the sea, and the land. Keep the stones where you will see and feel them often—in a pocket, on a bureau or bathroom counter, or on your desk.

Spell of Communication

This simple ritual empowers the participants to communicate clearly with one another. This spell uses the Eastern system of "chakras," referring to centers of energy in the body. In this system, the throat is associated with the color blue, and with communication, honesty, and relationship.

Because this is a meditation ritual, it's important to make your space as relaxing as possible. Reduce distractions, including turning off the telephone ringer. Wear comfortable clothing, in blue if possible. Avoid clothes that constrict or hide the throat.

Arrange comfortable armchairs or floor pillows facing one another on the floor. In between them, place a blue candle on an altar or table, high enough to be comfortably visible when seated, but not so high as to obscure your view of your partner.

This can be done as a meditation only, without divine aid. Simply follow your own custom for creating sacred space and then skip right to the meditation part. Here, however, we'll follow a Wiccan ritual format, invoking Mercury, the Roman god of communication, and his Celtic partner Rosmerta, goddess of domestic plenty. These two were worshiped as a divine couple in ancient times, depicted together as equals, with such symbols as ship's rudders, livestock, and overflowing purses.

(The ancients would never have invoked this pair for a ritual such as this, which draws on Eastern concepts and modern intentions. Such combinations of sources are common in Wicca; if your Paganism is more purist in its use of history, you will naturally want to adapt this ritual to suit your own preferences.)

On an altar at the north of your sacred space, place a picture, statue, or symbol of Mercury and Rosmerta, or just use two more blue candles to symbolize them.

First, the participants stand or sit, closing their eyes and thoroughly grounding and centering.

When you have finished, knock gently three times to signal to your partner that you are ready to begin.

One participant casts the circle by walking around it clockwise, starting in the north:

Let this circle be a place of safety.
Let this circle be a place of opening.
Let this circle be a place of love.

Another invokes the spirits of the four compass directions:

Spirits of the East, I do summon and call thee to guard this circle, and do charge thee to keep out all that stands in the way of our true words.

Spirits of the South, I do summon and call thee to guard this circle, and do charge thee to keep out all that stands in the way of our true courage.

Spirits of the West, I do summon and call thee to guard this circle, and do charge thee to keep out all that stands in the way of our true hearts.

Spirits of the North, I do summon and call thee to guard this circle, and do charge thee to keep out all that stands in the way of our true strength.

One participant invokes the goddess Rosmerta:

> Rosmerta, Goddess of Plenty, you who are equal to your partner and rule with him over the realm of communication, we ask your presence and your aid. Hail Rosmerta!

Another invokes the god Mercury:

> Mercury, God of Communication, you who are equal to your partner and rule with her over the realm of successful ventures, we ask your presence and your aid. Hail Mercury!

Next comes the heart of the ritual, the chakra meditation. You may wish to speak the words aloud in turn, each person echoing each step to reinforce its meaning. Other methods include memorizing the meditation or recording it on tape.

> I sit comfortably and briefly reconnect with the feeling of grounding and centering. I take a few deep breaths, feeling tension leave my body each time I exhale . . . I begin by concentrating on the back of my neck, relaxing my muscles and breathing into them. I am aware of a center of energy, a sphere of deep blue light at this part of my body. I let this sphere fill my consciousness and feel my awareness sinking into this place, opening and entering this realm. I may see a flower or other object here. If I do, I observe its condition, and see if it needs anything. I spend some time here, exploring and sensing. If I ask a question here, I can wait for the answer.

At this point, the participants fall silent for a few minutes so that each may concentrate on a personal experience. Knock gently on a chair or the floor to signal that you are ready to move on.

> Now I consciously flood the area with the same deep blue light, beautiful and true. I infuse my energy into this place, giving life and light to this part of myself. I remain here,

giving this blue essence to this place, until I feel it can accept
no more.

When you are ready, return to full consciousness and signal to your partner.

Open your eyes and spend a moment remembering what
you saw and felt, and thinking about what it meant to you.
At this point, partners may wish to share their experiences.
Otherwise, this can wait until after the ritual.

Stand, go to the altar, and speak aloud a promise to Mercury and Rosmerta:

O Ancient Ones, this day I do vow to speak my truth and
hear the truth of others.

You may wish to make other prayers and promises aloud
or silently.

The partners who invoked Mercury and Rosmerta each bid
farewell to them:

Mercury, God of Communication, we thank you for your
blessings and bid you farewell.

Rosmerta, Goddess of Plenty, we thank you for your blessings and bid you farewell.

Finally, dismiss the four directions and take down the
circle:

Spirits of the North [West, South, East], we thank you for
your protection and bid you farewell.

Let this space be cleansed and pure. So be it.

Four Points of Perspective

This simple Tarot exercise is not about solutions, but about
information. Here is where we seek to understand what we are
presenting to others. Many people are surprised to discover
how others view them and their situation.

The reader pulls four cards, using whatever method is comfortable. The four quadrants are interpreted as follows:

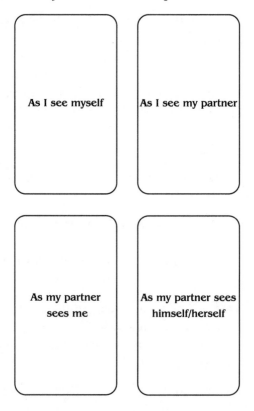

As I see myself

As I see my partner

As my partner sees me

As my partner sees himself/herself

This is a useful tool for working together but can also provide insight for situations in which a partner is unavailable physically or emotionally to work on improving the relationship. It does not provide any guidance for future action (that's up to you, with the best wisdom of your mind, heart, and spirit). This reading can be particularly useful in sorting out mixed feelings in complicated situations.

It may be helpful to do this exercise in a meditation or sacred space, and to spend some time in prayer or contemplation, using the card images to inspire your thinking about the emotions between you and your partner.

This exercise works best for relationships that involve you directly. If your situation involves more than one person, simply do the exercise again for your own relationship to each person. Return the cards to the deck and reshuffle after each reading.

Honesty Questions

This set of questions aims to help you get at your own emotional truth. The questions for chapter 3 closely reflect the discussion about the things that keep us from intimacy. After answering the questions, partners can meet to discuss their answers.

What am I ashamed of? Now? In the past? What happened that gave me the message that there is something basically wrong with me?

Whose feelings am I trying to take care of? Whose feelings have I tried to take care of in the past?

Where am I taking responsibility for other people's actions and needs? Whose actions and needs have I tried to take care of in the past?

How am I trying to be perfect? What am I trying to control? What have I done like this in the past?

How am I neglecting myself? How have I done this in the past?

What impressions am I trying to give? How am I trying to please people? Currently? In the past?

What am I afraid I won't have enough of? What am I afraid will happen? Now? In the past?

Ritual of Listening

When we realize that the simpler answers are not working, we begin to ask ourselves whether something else is going on within ourselves. The answer is almost always yes. We usually find that we have given away some portion of ourselves, and we need to reclaim and honor it. Often we discover that the part that is missing was given away long ago, perhaps even before we met our partners. If we really want to move beyond these barriers, we need to not only acknowledge our true selves, we need to communicate that to our partners and to know we have been heard.

This is not about agreeing, but about being heard and hearing. Sometimes agreements come out of the process, but this is about being, not doing.

Often disagreements and confrontations occur when one party feels misunderstood or simply "not heard." This can feel disrespectful, intimidating, or controlling. Frustration, anger, and resentment often follow. This discussion format, which we've labeled the Ritual of Listening, is meant to help people at a time when they see this anger and resentment either already coming between them or looming on the horizon.

Following this structure allows each person a chance for self-expression and a basis for knowing that one has been heard. It is meant for two people only, though in some cases it may be helpful to have a neutral third party present to help manage the process and add comments that facilitate listening. If your misunderstanding involves more than one other person, it is best to go through this process with each of them separately, focusing on your relationship with each of them rather than trying to manage their relationship with one another.

The Ritual of Listening works best if both parties agree to use it as directed. However, benefit can still be derived if only one person uses half of it. It is not a religious ritual, though spiritually oriented people may find it valuable to perform it in a religious context.

The format itself is very stiff and patterned, and may seem awkward at first. To derive the greatest benefit, participants should carefully consider what they wish to say to each other, perhaps even writing things down so that no important point will be forgotten. The Honesty Questions provide a helpful basis for coming up with the information you want to convey.

The Ritual of Listening requires being silent while the other person is talking. If you find it's difficult to break out of ordinary patterns of speech and interruption, it may help to use a "talking stick." It doesn't have to be a stick—any object will do. Whoever has the "stick" has the right to speak until he or she passes it to another.

The basic element of the format is a message communicated and understood:

1. One participant takes all the time he or she wants to make a statement.
2. The other listens *without interrupting* until he or she gets the talking stick. Then the listener restates what has been heard, *with no comment* on the truth or validity of the statement, using a neutral phrase such as "I hear you saying ————."
3. The first person receives the stick then adds any relevant information or corrects the listener's statement, and passes back the stick for another try at restating the message. They continue to do this until the listener is able to satisfy the speaker that he or she has been heard and understood.

In the Ritual of Listening, the participants—call them the Initiator and the Responder, roles that will stay consistent through this description—will engage in three rounds of listening, each with a slightly different focus.

Part 1. This part allows each person to have his or her complete say and to know that the other party has heard it. The partner does not have to agree or approve, simply to hear. The person who goes first, the Initiator, is usually the person starting the conversation or having the most obvious problem, though you can also decide who goes first by flipping a coin.

The Initiator says everything he or she wants to say about the current issue. They then follow the process above until the Initiator is satisfied that he or she has been heard.

Next, the process goes in the opposite direction. The Responder says everything he or she wants to say, for as long as it takes, without interruption, and it is the Initiator's job to restate until the Responder is sure of being heard.

The two then remain still for *sixty seconds of silence.*

Part 2.   Here the Initiator and the Responder have a chance to process the information they've received.

The Responder (who went second in the first part) begins by describing what is similar in their two statements, delivering these observations without interruption. The Initiator restates these observations until the Responder is sure of being heard.

Then the process happens again in reverse. The Initiator (who went first in the first part) begins by describing what he or she sees as similarities in what they both said, and it is the Responder's job to restate the Initiator's words until the Initiator is satisfied that he or she was heard.

The two then pause for *sixty seconds of silence.*

Part 3.   In this part, the participants use creativity and dreaming to break out of old thought and action ruts that may have contributed to the issues before them. Instead of demanding things of each other, they make wishes, and thereby create a basis for dialogue.

The Initiator begins by saying, without interruption, what would happen if he or she could wave a magic wand and make any wish come true. Next, the talking stick goes to the Responder. The Responder restates the Initiator's wish, going back and forth until the Initiator believes he or she was heard.

Finally the Responder describes, without interruption, what would happen if he or she could wave a magic wand, then passes the stick to the Initiator. The Initiator restates the message until the Responder is sure of being heard.

The participants then remain still for *sixty seconds of silence.*

Part 4.   By this time, it should be apparent where there are areas of substantial agreement and where there are not. If needed, finish the discussion with specific actions to be taken.

Handfasting

This is written as a marriage ceremony, but may be easily altered for couples who are not choosing to wed, for a same-sex union, or for a ceremony uniting more than two people.

Celebrant. "Friends, we are gathered in the presence of Nature Herself to witness the joining together of ———— and ————. Let us begin by asking Divine blessings on this time."

> Spirits of the East, bring us light. Illumine, guard, and guide this gathering, clearing our minds and increasing our understanding. Be here now.
>
> Spirits of the South, bring us fire. Enflame, guard, and guide this gathering with a sense of purpose and passion. Be here now.
>
> Spirits of the West, bring us the waters of life. Cradle, guard, and guide this gathering, bringing us into a new and beautiful relationship with one another. Be here now.
>
> Spirits of the North, bring us the good things of this world. Nurture, guard, and guide this gathering that we may know the abundance of life and love. Be here now.

Celebrant. "The circle is cast. We stand between the worlds on sacred ground. God of Life, Goddess of Love, be here as you have created us for one another. Ancestors of flesh and spirit, be here as witnesses. Strengthen the ties that hold us together.

"———— and ———— have come to give themselves to one

another in this holy covenant, a recognition of a bond that was forged and honored between them long before this day.

"We welcome you, ——— and ———, to this moment in your lives, and gratefully acknowledge the place you have in one another's hearts. We have gathered here for a holy purpose, to witness this covenant. We represent all those whom you have loved, and who have loved you, and all those whom you will love and who will love you. And we offer our prayers that you might be blessed beyond your imagining.

"We ask the spirits of their home, the gods of this place, and the Gods of our worship to do all in your power to uphold, nurture, and care for ——— and ———'s growth as individuals, as loving partners, and as friends. And we as their witnesses pledge the same."

(Officiants and witnesses each lay hands on the heads of the partners in turn, and give personal blessings to them.)

Celebrant. "I ask you now to declare your intention to enter into union with one another."

(To each partner in turn)

"———, will you take ——— to live together in sacred marriage? If so, say 'I will.'

"Will you offer your love, comfort, nurturing, honesty, blessing, and honor, in sickness and health, in times of darkness and light, so long as your love shall endure? If so, say 'I will.' "

(To each partner in turn)

"———, please repeat after me."

> ———, I vow that I shall honor the east by honoring you as my equal.
> ———, I vow that I shall honor the south by choosing our paths in consensus.
> ———, I vow that I shall honor the west by being emotionally honest in our relationship.
> ———, I vow that I shall honor the north by freely giving to you and by freely receiving from you.

————, I vow that I shall honor the Divine within you by
loving you and by making our relationship primary.

Celebrant. "Please face one another and join hands. In a
tradition older than history, we bind your hands fast together
with this cord. It is a symbol of the new thing that is manifest
when you speak your vows to one another. It is a symbol of
your unity, a triple cord that is very strong."
(To each partner in turn)
"Please repeat after me."

I ————, take you, ————, to my hand, my heart, and my
spirit, to have and to hold from this day forward, for better,
for worse, for richer, for poorer, in sickness and in health, in
joy and sorrow, to love and to cherish, until our love shall
end.

Celebrant. "What do you bring as a gift for one another?
These gifts are the outward and visible sign of an inward and
spiritual bond and grace. May they who receive them continue
in peace, love, wisdom, and good fortune all the days of their
lives."
(To each partner in turn)
"————, please give ———— your gift, and repeat after me."

————, I give you ———— as a sign of my vow and with all
that I am and all that I have I honor you. I give you my
promise that from this day forward you shall not walk alone.
My heart will be your shelter. My arms will be your home.
My face will turn first to you. My spirit will comfort you. I
am honored to be your [wife/husband/love] and it is my joy
to make this vow.

Celebrant. "You have declared your consent and your vow
before the Givers of Life and Love. May your covenant be confirmed and fill you both with grace and love.
"May the power of their covenant, the look of love in their

eyes, and the depth of commitment to each other grow and blossom for all to see. We thank you, Givers of Life and Love, for your presence and witness this day and ask that you continue to bless ——— and ———.

"Therefore, ——— and ———, go forth into this world. Where there is hatred, sow love, where there is injury, bring pardon, where there is doubt, sow faith, and where there is despair, bring hope. The good wishes of we here present go with you. So be it!"

Altar of Growth and Healing

To do this, you first need to set up an altar. It can be very simple—a few stones piled up with a reasonably flat surface on top, or even just an area of earth set aside. If you don't have outdoor space, use a space on a shelf, table, or windowsill. The altar should be large enough to include at least two plants, and it should be somewhere that gets a good amount of sunlight.

Next, each person doing the ritual should choose a plant to represent himself or herself. This choice should reflect your current emotional state, not an idealized version. Along with your heart, consider your climate and soil, and any herbal, magical, or divine associations you have for specific plants. If you do this ritual in the winter, you may wish to select and empower plants that can be set into the ground in the spring.

When your altar is ready, and as soon as possible after obtaining your plants, arrange for some private time near your altar. Bring a trowel or spade for planting, some water, some birdseed, and a chalice of wine or juice.

Spend a moment or two grounding and centering. Then ask the blessings of the place upon your work:

> Spirits of this place, we gather here to perform a rite of healing and growth. We call you, by whatever name you wish to be called, to witness and bless our ritual, and accept our offerings.

Each participant places a small amount of birdseed on the altar in offering. (If you're indoors, scatter the seeds outside after the ritual.)

Choose one plant to be planted first. The person associated with that plant holds or touches it and offers this prayer:

Fruitful Land, I ask your blessings of nourishment and foundation for me and for this green life.

Gentle Rain, I ask your blessings of cleansing and nurturing for me and for this green life.

Warm Sun, I ask your blessings of light and growth for me and for this green life.

Add any other prayers you feel are appropriate, to the gods and goddesses of your personal faith or to those entities most closely connected with the healing work you are doing for yourself.

A partner, meanwhile, looks to the new home of this plant, digging a hole or trench and otherwise creating its home. When the site is ready, the partner says:

As this plant grows, so may healing grow in you, and in all that you touch.

The one holding the plant places it in the ground:

Into this earth I place my hopes for healing! [Add a sentence or two expressing your hopes in your own words.] May the earth receive my hopes and bring them to life! So may it be done!

The partner echoes "So may it be done!" Together they make sure it is well situated and watered. Repeat for each plant.

When the altar garden is planted, face each other and hold the chalice between you. Each partner takes a sip from the cup and says:

I drink to you and to me, to your growth and mine. As we share this cup, let us share this garden and tend it to the best of our ability. This I pledge to you in love and trust, with my true heart.

Add any personal toasts or prayers, then pour the rest of the cup onto the earth in offering.

As time goes by, place objects on the altar that remind you of your own healing work and of the growth of your relationship. Tend the plants as well as you can, and accept that they, like you, have cycles of health and sickness, birth and death.

Centering Worksheet

Try filling out this Centering Worksheet every day. Set aside a few moments before you go to bed. Writing down your goals and achievements works better than just thinking about them, forcing you to give yourself the acknowledgments you might be tempted to gloss over while you concentrate on your failures.

At the end of the day, look at yesterday's list and answer yes or no to the question of "Did I do this?" You will move closer to your own center of strength with each check mark for a yes answer. Don't let yourself feel guilty or self-critical over the things that aren't done. You're not trying to earn an A+ here. If you hit 80 percent of your goals over several weeks, that's great. If you don't, consider whether you're setting your standards too high, and check your goals to make sure they're manageable.

The most important part of the worksheet, however, is the last part: your gratitudes. These must be different every day. This forces you to look at each day as a unique gift, though you can repeat subjects. For instance, one day you can be grateful that a relative called to talk about his job. The next day you can be grateful that he *has* a job.

Save the sheets if you like. You'll be amazed at what you have accomplished in a few days! Then select some things for the next day.

If you can sustain this every day for three weeks, it is likely to become a habit you can use to keep yourself centered regularly. If you don't manage this, don't criticize yourself—remember that you have this tool and can return to it when you find yourself losing your centering.

DAILY CENTERING WORKSHEET
DATE ———

Today, for my personal care, I need to:
- ☐ 1.
- ☐ 2.
- ☐ 3.

Today, for living in general, I need to:
- ☐ 1.
- ☐ 2.
- ☐ 3.

Today, for my work, I need to:
- ☐ 1.
- ☐ 2.
- ☐ 3.

Today, for my world, I need to:
- ☐ 1. (Family)
- ☐ 2. (Friend)
- ☐ 3. (World)

Today I am grateful for these twenty things:

_____

_____

_____

_____

_____

_____

_____

_____

Conquering Inner Obstacles

Trying things on.   When we're making choices, we test our own wishes against our inner voice and against common courtesy. If we wish to see ourselves in a particular way, we "try it on" to see how it feels to us. Recently, Cynthia has been working with herself as a visual artist. So she tried on this sentence: "I, Cynthia Jane Collins, am a beautiful and fruitful painter."

Choose a sentence for yourself—something you want to try on, representing a positive way of seeing you. Write down your sentence.

Take a moment to listen to the first reactions that come into your mind, to the voice of your inner critic or censor. These thoughts may have to do with why this vision won't work for you or this goal won't be achievable. Immediately counter each reaction from the inner critic with another sentence that answers that objection.

For instance, after Cynthia wrote her first "I am" sentence, she heard her inner critic say, "But you don't paint like ———." Her counter voice was "I paint just exactly like myself. My work looks exactly like my work."

Repeat the process—writing down the sentence, listening for the inner critic, and countering its objections—a dozen or so times.

Twenty-four-hour test.   This is another way to try things on. Suppose you have just been offered a new job. Should you take it or not? Pretend for twenty-four hours that you have absolutely decided yes, and note your reactions. Then pretend for twenty-four hours that you have absolutely decided no, and see what comes up then. Your answer should become more clear.

Forty-eight-hour rule.   This is an exercise to try when you are very angry with someone. (If the person in question is causing immediate harm to you or others, don't do this exercise unless all steps have been taken to stop the harm from happening.) Wait forty-eight hours before confronting the person about the problem. During that time, ask yourself these questions:

- *What is going on for you?*   Not just in the situation, but in general. It is helpful to write this answer by hand, expressing what really comes into your head without trying to edit it, making it sound nice or even spelling it correctly. Scribble it if that seems right.
- *How does the other person in this situation view himself or herself in a favorable light?*   Having expressed your anger and other feelings, figure out as best you can what's going on for the other person, how he or she justifies the actions or words that are making you angry.
- *Have you violated your own ethics?*   If you have, the violation often includes making assumptions about other people, in not giving and receiving freely. When you assume things about other people, when you expect compensation for your gifts and feel obligated to make up for what you receive, you harm yourself.

With these questions answered, you have the start of the information you need to make good decisions about what you can and cannot give and receive.

Centering Tarot Spread

This Tarot spread is especially valuable at moments of crossroads or decision making. It is also useful at pivotal points in a long process or project.

First, draw a card and place it in the center of your reading area. This is *where you are now.*

Next, place one card below and to the left of the center card. This is *what you resent.*

Then place a card below and to the right of the center card. This is *what you are grateful for.*

Place a card between the last two cards. This is *what will help you move from resentment to gratitude.*

Next, place one card above and to the left of the center card. This is *what you fear.*

Then place another card above and to the right of the center card. This is *what you love.*

Finally, place a card between the last two cards. This is *what will help you move from fear to love.*

Handparting

Celebrant prepares the altar with symbols of healing and individual strength, then casts the circle with the couple inside and calls upon whatever gods and goddesses were invoked at the original handfasting.

Celebrant. "Spirits of the Four Directions, [names of gods and goddesses], and all who are here, seen and unseen, I call you this day to witness the parting of the hands of ——— and ———.

"——— and ———, step forward and join hands."

(To each in turn)

"———, what are the lessons you learned in this relationship?" (Each is given a few moments to answer.)

(To each in turn)

"———, what are you grateful for from this partnership?" (Each is given a few moments to answer.)

Celebrant. "When you were bound together before the gods of your worship, you promised yourselves to one another for as long as your love should last. Has the time come when that love is at an end?" The partners must agree. (If one does not, the ritual is ended and the celebrant assists the couple in working toward consensus on the question.)

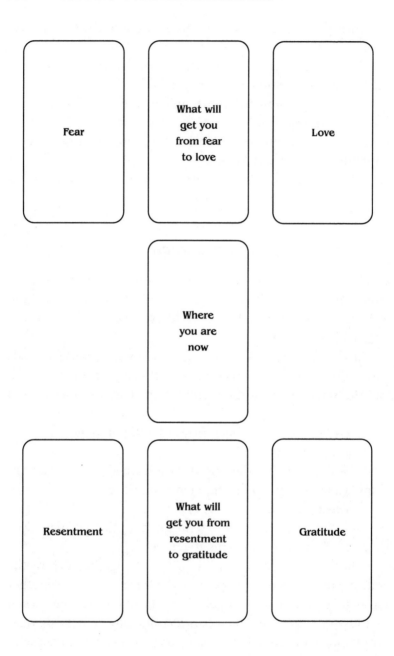

Celebrant then takes the partners' hands and pulls them apart, moving them away from one another.

(To each in turn)

Celebrant. "————, I ask you now to return the token you received from your partner at handfasting." They return their rings or other tokens.

(To each in turn)

"Repeat after me."

I, ————, do release you, ————, from the love we have shared. On my honor, and before these witnesses, seen and unseen, I pledge to speak no ill of you, and to meet you in the future with respect and friendship. I wish you healing and happiness as a free person.

Celebrant. "It is done. Gods and Goddesses, Spirits of this place, Watchers of the Four Directions, I call on you to witness the parting of these hands, and to recognize ———— and ———— as free and independent souls. So be it."

Celebrant bids farewell to the Goddesses and Gods and takes down the circle.

Centering Meditation

Close your eyes. Be still. Breathe deep. Align your body so that it is comfortable, straight but loose. As you breathe, focus your attention to the top of your head, and visualize a swirling sphere of energy above you. This is your point of contact with the divine. Focus on it for a few moments.

On an in-breath, feel the energy begin to emanate downward into your body, slowly moving downward, filling you and your aura with shimmering white light, with the energy of the skies. Slowly pull this energy downward, into your head . . . then into your neck . . . then into your chest . . . toward your heart. Feel the energy flow out through your shoulders

. . . into your arms . . . down to your hands, and to the tips of your fingers. As you breathe, feel it flow down through your stomach area, toward your hips and your genitals, and farther down, into your legs, toward your knees. See the swirling light fill your entire aura, down past the bottoms of your feet.

Feel the solid contact between your feet and the earth. Reach downward with your mind, pushing the energy down past the place where you're standing, deep down into the fruitful earth itself.

Then, as you breathe in, feel the green, nurturing energy of the earth flow upward into you, again filling you and your aura with light. Up into your feet . . . past your knees . . . into your hips . . . up to your genitals . . . toward your stomach. Pull the light slowly upward to your lungs and your breast, out along your arms, up toward your neck. Feel the energy reach upward to the top of your head, and filter up toward the stars.

Spend a few moments breathing deeply, seeing yourself at the intersection of two great streams of energy, which cleanse you and renew you.

Giving and Receiving Incense

1 part catnip, for happiness
1 part dandelion fluff, for wishes
1 part periwinkle petals, for friendship and safety

Marbles

This exercise empowers ordinary marbles as a divinatory tool for recognizing and understanding anger. It doesn't tell you what to do with that anger, but it may help you to think about it in more productive ways.

Choose six marbles.   One red, one yellow, one green, and three of a neutral color such as blue or white.

Magically cleanse the marbles as follows: Hold them in your receiving hand (see introduction for an explanation of this). Breathe deeply as you visualize the energy of the earth coming up from the ground, through your feet and legs, into your body. Draw the energy into the hand with the marbles, allowing it to pass through the marbles and back down to the earth until the marbles "feel" clean and clear.

Other methods of cleansing: Place the marbles in a container of salt to ritually cleanse them. Leave them outside for a night during the waning moon (so that any residual energy is dissipated).

After you are satisfied that the marbles are clear and clean, surround yourself with a protective circle. Offer the marbles to each of the quarters and to the center, saying something such as: "I offer these for sacred use. Protect them and me from all abuse."

Assign and seal the energies of the marbles.   Take the three neutral-colored marbles one at a time in your sending hand and begin to focus, imagining that you are sending neutral energy to each one. When each marble feels invested, pass your sending hand three times sunwise (clockwise) over it, saying: "This tool is sealed and sacred to me: As I will, so mote it be."

Select the green marble, placing it your sending hand. Call to mind things that exemplify green anger for you, send the energy into the marble. The clearer your images and examples, the stronger the "charge." When the green marble feels "full," pass your sending hand three times sunwise over it, saying: "This tool is sealed and sacred to me: As I will, so mote it be." Then set it aside. Do the same with the yellow marble using yellow anger, then the red one using red anger. Keep the marbles in a small pouch or container.

Divination.   If you suspect that anger has a part in what you are dealing with, pick a marble at random, then return it to the pouch and shake it to mix up the marbles. Do this a total of three times.

If done with sincere intent, calling on whatever source of spiritual inspiration you feel is appropriate, this can function as a divination, with the combinations indicating directions to explore as you figure out what's going on for you.

Three of any color. This is very important and needs immediate attention! Look at what kind of anger is represented and match the feelings to your situation.

Two of any color. This is important. Again, match the feelings to the situation but realize that it may not yet be time to act.

One of any color. Something here may need to be considered in the future.

All neutral. Anger is not something that needs to concern you at this time or you have already identified the problems.

Balance Tarot Spread

This Tarot spread is really two readings, the first observing a situation and the second offering advice.

On the left side of your space, lay a card for the current situation and another below it for the foundation of that situation. Toward the right, lay a card for East/Equals, then three more cards in a clockwise compass for South/Consensus, West/Emotional Honesty, and North/Giving and Receiving. In the center goes a final card for balance.

Read all these cards and glean whatever information you see in them, making notes if you like. The cards of the compass reflect what's currently going on for you in relation to the five Principles of this book.

Next, choose one of the cards of the compass to form the foundation of the second part of the reading. This should be the direction, area, or principle that is of most concern. To help

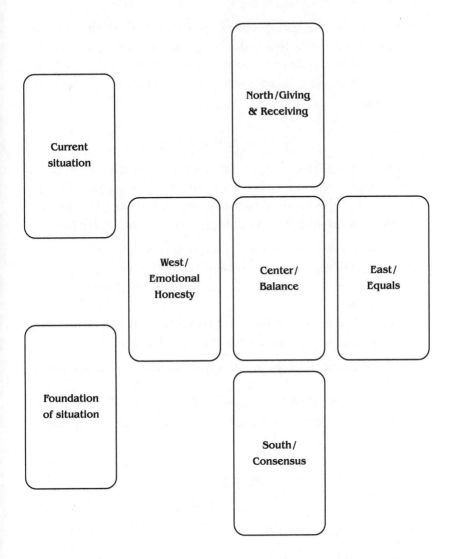

you decide which one to pick, look for reversed cards first, then look for Major Arcana cards. If there is more than one reversed card, choose a reversed Major Arcana first, or the one with the lowest number. If there are two of the same value (two reversed Aces, for example), use them both.

Once you've chosen one, pick up that card and move it to

the bottom of the space. Return the other cards to the bottom of the deck, and without shuffling, lay out four more cards above it. Use the advice cards to help you decide on actions that will bring you closer to the balance indicated on the outcome card.

Fivefold Blessing

Create a sacred space according to your custom. Remove your robes if that is comfortable for everyone. One partner kneels and delivers the Fivefold Blessing, bestowing each kiss before speaking and rising to a standing position at the fourth line:

> Blessed be thy feet, that have brought thee to this place
> Blessed be thy knees, which kneel before the sacred altar
> Blessed be thy [womb/phallus], without which we would
>   not be
> Blessed be thy breast, formed in beauty and strength
> Blessed be thy lips, which utter the sacred names

Then the kiss flows in the other direction with the same words.

This simple blessing can be performed by more than two partners by making sure each person gets a chance to bless each other person.

Three Buttons

This is an effective ritual and exercise that empowers small symbols to express anger and start a conversation without "picking a fight."

The symbols don't have to be buttons—you can use any small object. Each person chooses three of the same object. Magically cleanse their symbols, as in the Marbles exercise above, then offer this prayer:

> Goddess and God of love and choice,
> Let these symbols be my voice

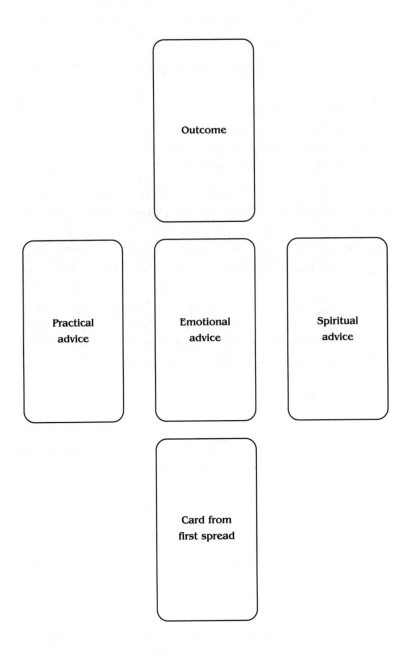

Give them the power to speak for me
With truth and faith and clarity

Trade buttons so that you are holding your partner's three symbols:

Goddess and God of love set free
I accept these symbols to speak to me
Guide me in wisdom that I may hear
Renew my heart and keep it clear

If you have more than one partner, repeat the second prayer to accept the symbols of each person. Take back your three buttons. Choose a space for each of you that you see every day—most people use a bureau, but an altar, desk, night table, or even the dashboard of the car can work. If you are angry, place one, two, or three on the other person's space. One button means "I'm slightly upset, let's talk when you get a chance." Two buttons mean "Something's starting to bother me, and I need to talk about it." Three buttons mean "I'm seriously angry and I need to talk as soon as possible!"

The Simplest Love Spell of All

This spell by Jane Raeburn (first printed in Lilith McClelland's *Salem Witches' Book of Love Spells*) was originally intended for those seeking to attract a new lover, but may be easily adapted to invoke love for oneself or renew an existing love:

You'll need a red candle and nonflammable candleholder, plus patchouli oil, cinnamon oil, rose oil, or all three.

First, make sure you're really ready for a new love, that you've gotten over the hurts of the past, and are ready for fresh energy in your lovelife.

Anoint the red candle with patchouli (for a passionate relationship), cinnamon (for an affectionate, balanced relationship), or rose (for abiding love). Hold it in your hands and close your eyes as you enter a meditative state.

When you feel connected to your source of inspiration, begin visualizing yourself enjoying a new love. Don't imagine any details—you don't want to close off any possibilities, or you might miss out on something wonderful! Instead, see yourself doing the things you would do with a partner: walking, dining, playing sports, going to cultural events, worshiping, shopping, snuggling, reading, making love. See yourself filled with delight, giving and receiving.

Say these words:

"I open my heart to a new love. I open my mind to a new love. I open my soul to a new love."

Pray to the deity of your choice:

"Venus [or God or Allah or Mother Earth], help me to be truly open to a new love. Help me to be the best person I can be, so I may be worthy of such a love."

Describe the sort of love you seek, being careful to describe a relationship rather than a person.

"I place this quest in Your hands, and trust you to bring it to fruition, with harm to none and in keeping with my fate."

As you say this last sentence, put the candle in the holder. As you make this gesture, mentally place your search in the deity's keeping. Light the candle and let it burn all night in a safe place, away from kids or pets. When you awake, know that your deity is looking after your search for love. Concentrate on doing the things that renew and awaken you. Take up a new creative project, finish an old one, cut out a bad habit, see friends who energize you, limit your time with people who drain you. Challenge yourself to be an interesting, thoughtful, confident person. Know that love will follow.

Resources

One book can never cover all aspects of a subject as big as partnership and relationship. Here, we list a few of the books that have inspired and informed us as we created this volume. They are organized in groups of three to help you further explore the subjects were covered here.

Three Books for Learning about Oneself

The Dance of Anger (New York: HarperPerennial, 1989).
The Dance of Intimacy (New York: HarperPerennial, 1990).
The Dance of Deception (New York: HarperPerennial, 1994).

These three books by Harriet Lerner are useful and accessible guides. *The Dance of Anger* is a challenging book that discusses ways anger manifests in our lives, and ways to use the power in that anger for constructive change. *The Dance of Inti-*

macy offers practical ideas on learning how to be oneself while staying connected to families and friends. *The Dance of Deception* explores the ways we are deceived as well as how we deceive others and ourselves.

Three Books about Making Sense of Our Past

Adult Children: Secrets of Dysfunctional Families, John and Linda Friel (Deerfield Beach, Fla.: Health Communications, 1988).

A simple and comprehensive look at how we are trained as children to function as adults and how that can get in the way of expressing our true selves. While the authors tend to be a bit global, their points are well taken.

Genograms in Family Assessment, Monica McGoldrick and Randy Gerson (New York: Norton, 1985).

This practical book offers simple ways to identify and graph family traits and functions. If you enjoy genealogy, or are simply curious about your family, this book is wonderful.

The Courage to Heal: A Guide for Women Survivors of Sexual Abuse, Ellen Bass and Laura Davis (New York: HarperPerennial, 1994).

The ground-breaking book on stages of healing after sexual abuse.

Three Books about Relating to Other People

The Fragile Bond: In Search of an Intimate, Equal and Enduring Marriage, Augustus Y. Napier (New York: HarperCollins, 1990).

A very useful book about dealing with the obstacles to equality and intimacy in a committed partnership.

Unholy Hungers: Encountering the Psychic Vampire in Ourselves and Others, Barbara Hort (Boston: Shambhala, 1996).

This is a Jungian exploration of how the archetype of the vampire functions in our lives and the lives of those around us.

Wicca Covens: How to Start and Organize Your Own, Judy Harrow (New York: Citadel, 1999).

The dynamics of relationship among Wiccans, with an excellent exposition of common problems.

Three Books about Codependence

Codependence: Misunderstood and Mistreated, Anne Wilson Schaef (San Francisco: HarperSanFrancisco, 1986).

This is a careful, somewhat clinical look at the underlying process of addictions and codependence. It includes an excellent section on the traits of the codependent, though painted with a somewhat broad brush.

Codependent No More, Melody Beattie (New York: MJF Books, Fine Communications, 1987).

This is a basic course on "cleaning up your side of the street" while allowing others to do the same.

A Codependent's Guide to the 12 Steps, Melody Beattie (New York: Prentice Hall Parkside, 1990).

Based on the 12 steps of Alcoholics Anonymous, this book offers a structured way to begin a program of recovery from codependent behaviors. Includes exercises that may be helpful to individuals or groups.

Three Books about Pagan Religions

Contemporary Paganism: Listening People, Speaking Earth, Graham Harvey (New York: New York University Press, 1997).

A religious studies scholar depicts some of the basic flavors of Paganism. Harvey's information is oriented toward the United Kingdom but has value for its focus on the wide variety of Pagan expressions.

Drawing Down the Moon, Margot Adler (New York: Penguin USA, 1997).

A journalist and Wiccan writes about the reality of today's Pagans. Somewhat dated, but still a thoughtful perspective.

The Spiral Dance, Starhawk (San Francisco: HarperSanFrancisco, 1979, 1989, 1999).

This is the classic look at emerging contemporary Wicca, with a strong feminist slant. It includes explanations, spellwork, ritual and various exercises.

Three Books about Pagan Spells and Rituals

Spell Craft, Lilith McClelland (Chicago: Eschaton, 1997).

This book is aimed at younger practitioners but provides a reliable, ethical introduction for all ages.

The Spell of Making, Blacksun (Chicago: Eschaton, 1996).

Consists chiefly of an account of the preparation of one ritual. Useful as an introduction to how Pagans create their ceremonies.

Celtic Wicca, Jane Raeburn (New York: Citadel Press, 2001).

Okay, this was written by one of your humble authors, but it also includes a detailed chapter on creating a ritual with reference to historical information.

Three Books about Tarot

The Complete Idiot's Guide to Tarot and Fortune Telling, Arlene Tognetti and Lisa Lenard and Dennis Flaherty (New York: Alpha Books, 1998).

An excellent introduction with good organization, presentation and practical examples.

Tarot and Individuation: Correspondences with Cabala and Alchemy, Irene Gad (York, Me.: Weiser, 1994).

A very interesting weaving of psychological theory, symbolism and magic toward the goal of knowing oneself better through study of the Major Arcana.

Jung and the Tarot, Sallie Nichols (York, Me.: Weiser, 1980).

A classic study of the historical roots of Tarot imagery from a Jungian perspective. Very strong on archetypes and symbolism for one's life journey.

Three Books of Special Interest to Women

The Metamorphosis of Baubo: Myths about Women's Sexual Energy, Winifred Milius Lubell (Nashville, Tenn.: Vanderbilt University Press, 1994).

A delightful and well-researched book that celebrates the reality of women's sexuality and strength in the person of the goddess Baubo.

Women's Reality, Anne Wilson Schaef (San Francisco: HarperSanFrancisco, 1981, 1992).

A life-changing look at how popular culture has taken away the voices of women and other groups. This early work is as relevant today as it was when it was written 20 years ago. If you doubt it, watch one hour of children's television.

Fat Is a Feminist Issue II, Susie Orbach (New York: Berkley Books, 1982, 1987).

This is a rare case where the author's second treatment of the same subject is better than her first. Building on the information in the first book, this one offers a compassionate and simple revolutionary way to look at and take care of our bodies.

Three Books of Special Interest to Men

Knights Without Armor: A Practical Guide for Men in Quest of the Masculine Soul, Aaron Kipnis (Los Angeles: J. P. Tarcher, 1991).

An allegory describing men's journey toward spiritual development, wholeness and emotional growth.

Victims No Longer: Men Recovering from Incest and Other Child Abuse, Mike Lew and Ellen Bass (New York: HarperCollins, 1990).
Aimed at male survivors of sexual abuse, this book offers concrete suggestions for becoming whole.

Gods in Everyman, Jean Shinoda Bolen (New York: HarperCollins, 1990).
A look at Jungian archetypes of the male, describing the strengths and weaknesses of each.

Three Resources on Substance Abuse

When Society Becomes an Addict, Anne Wilson Schaef (San Francisco: HarperSanFrancisco, 1988).
A look at how our culture exemplifies the traits of the process and substance abuser. Particularly poignant regarding work situations.

"Stepping Through to Recovery," Anodea Judith (first published in *Green Egg*, Ostara 1991; access online at http://members.aol.com/JehanaS/recovery.html).
Article offers a Pagan spiritual outlook on the twelve steps of Alcoholics Anonymous and similar groups.

"Pagans in Recovery Resource Packet," Selena Fox. (Order online through www.circlesanctuary.org.)
A brief summary of her work in this area.

Three Books about Pagan Ethics

Dreaming the Dark: Magic, Sex and Politics, Starhawk (Boston: Beacon, 1997).

A visionary look the intersection of Wiccan ethics and Western culture.

Wiccan Warrior: Walking a Spiritual Path in a Sometimes Hostile World, Kerr Cuhulain (St. Paul, Minn: Llewellyn, 2000).

Cuhulain, a police officer and military veteran brings together heroic and warrior traditions of many cultures for a revitalized Western spirituality that rejects dogma and hierarchy, making each person his or her own hero.

When . . . Why . . . If, Robin Wood (Dearborn, Mich. Livingtree, 1997).

A Pagan artist's personal view from the front lines of Pagan ethical issues.

Three Useful Books on World Mythology

Hero with a Thousand Faces, Joseph Campbell (Princeton, N.J.: Princeton University Press, 1972).

An inspiring, if somewhat heavily male-oriented, work that tells us the story behind the stories we tell. Famous as the inspiration for *Star Wars,* but important to understanding myth and storytelling in many forms.

Myths and Symbols in Pagan Europe: Early Scandinavian and Celtic Religions, Hilda Roderick Ellis Davidson (Syracuse, N.Y.: Syracuse University Press, 1989).

Especially useful for the parallels it draws between the two cultures.

The Golden Bough, James George Frazer (many editions available, but one recent one is New York: Simon & Schuster, 1996).

Most of Frazer's conclusions are outdated, yet his retelling of myths themselves have made this book a useful resource for Pagans and other students of myth.

Index

About the Authors

CYNTHIA JANE COLLINS holds a master of divinity degree from Christian Theological Seminary and a master of science degree in counseling (Phi Kappa Phi) from the University of Evansville. She is a clinical member of the American Association for Marriage and Family Therapy, and is licensed to practice in her home state of Maine. She is a founding member and high priestess in the Silver Cauldron coven.

She has at various times held offices in the Mental Health Association, Kiwanis, community, and clergy associations and EarthTides Pagan Network. She has produced and directed a radio show, appeared on *Geraldo* as an expert in mental health, and presented many workshops and seminars, including a Wiccan training program, Vacation Pagan School.

She is a visual artist whose paintings have appeared in a number of exhibitions, and is a collector of many things that sparkle or shine. She is known to be partial to children (hers are Lee, Sam, and Steph, plus Steph's husband Dave) and pets (someone else's), books (everyone's), the ocean, and chocolate in most forms.

JANE RAEBURN got her first journalism job at age nineteen and has been working with words ever since, most recently as a Web site producer. She first drew attention in the Pagan community with "Jane's Tidings," a column of Pagan- and Wiccan-related news that she wrote for seven years. She has also published articles on such aspects of Pagan life as dealing with the media and Wiccan house-hunting.

Her first book, *Celtic Wicca: Ancient Wisdom for the 21ˢᵗ Century*, was published by Citadel Press in 2001. In it, Raeburn seeks to provide a living spiritual path that respects the facts of Celtic history. Her next book will be a Pagan poetry anthology, tentatively titled *The Pagan's Muse.*

She is a trained Wiccan priestess and is active in Maine Pagan circles, most notably as moderator of a popular and long-running e-mail forum for Maine Pagans. She also plays recorder in an early-music group. She is high priestess of the Temple of Brigantia, a Celto-Roman group she founded with her husband Cassius. They live in Maine with three cats, a dog, and a lizard.